A Wild Haruki Chase

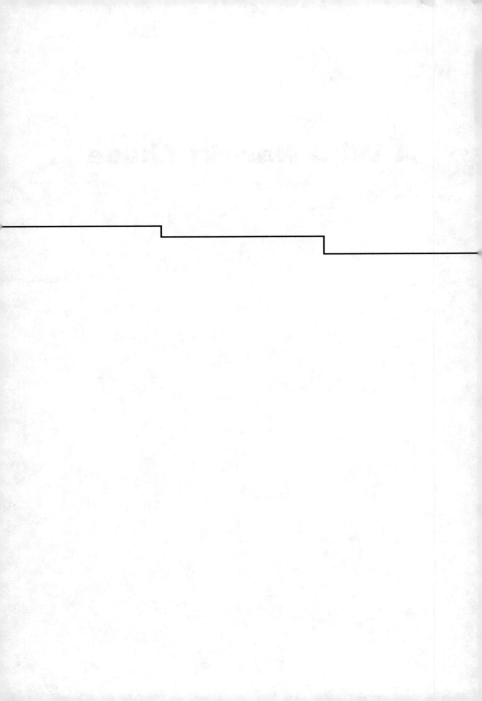

A Wild Haruki Chase
Reading Murakami Around the World

**Compiled and translated
by The Japan Foundation**

JAPANFOUNDATION

Stone Bridge Press • Berkeley, California

Published by
Stone Bridge Press
P. O. Box 8208
Berkeley, CA 94707
tel 510-524-8732 • www.stonebridge.com • sbp@stonebridge.com

This publication was generously supported by a grant from The Japan Foundation.

This anthology was planned and compiled by The Japan Foundation based on special feature articles carried in its bimonthly Japanese-language culture magazine, *Wochi Kochi,* vol. 12 (August/September 2006), with the addition of several articles newly written for this publication.

Compiled and translated by The Japan Foundation
Ark Mori Bldg., 1-12-32 Akasaka, Minato-ku
Tokyo 107-6021, Japan

The Japanese text was translated by the following contributors:
Kay Yokota, Nozomu Kawamoto, WordCraft.

LIBRARY OF CONGRESS CATALOGING-IN-PUBLICATION DATA
A wild Haruki chase : reading Murakami around the world / compiled and translated by the Japan Foundation.
    p. cm.
  Based on special feature articles appearing in "Wochi kochi, vol. 12, with some additional articles newly written; the Japanese text translated into English.
  ISBN 978-1-933330-66-2 (pbk.)
  1. Murakami, Haruki, 1949—Appreciation. I. Kokusai Koryu Kikin.
PL856.U673Z898 2008
895.6'35—dc22

                          2008007976

Contents

Introduction
The Murakami Aeroplain

Jay Rubin

I don't know if this is true of most people, but I tend
to go through the day, every day, with some kind of
music playing in the background—not live music that
other people can hear, but sounds in my brain, usually
recollected tunes that I have heard recently. (I don't like
"background music" as such: when I listen to music, I
listen, I don't do other things.) During the past week or
so, most of the melodies in my brain have come from
a CD I was given in Copenhagen by the composer

Massimo Fiorentino, who was born in Naples, Italy in 1973 but grew up in Denmark. I had the good fortune to cross paths with Massimo on the evening of September 28, 2006, when he attended an informal talk I gave to the Denmark-Japan Society on the subject of translating Haruki Murakami. I had just flown in that day from Dublin, where I had seen an amazingly precise model of a Viking ship in the National Museum of Ireland and learned that Dublin was founded in 841 by the Vikings, who gave it the name *Dubh Linn* (black pool). A few days later I would visit the Viking Ship Museum in Roskilde, where I would see the actual re-assembled fragments of an amazingly similar Viking ship that had originally been built in Dublin and made the voyage across the North Sea before it was sunk in the Roskilde fjord. Dublin was the second stop I was making with my wife on a trip that began in Seattle, Washington and had its first destination in Cork, Ireland, the city where Haruki Murakami was announced as the winner of the Frank O'Connor International Short Story Award on the evening of September 24. Our third destination was Copenhagen to visit Mette Holm, the Danish translator of Murakami, whom we had met that March in Tokyo at the international Murakami symposium. Ms. Holm was the one who had arranged for me to talk at the Denmark-Japan Society, where Massimo Fiorentino handed me his CD, titled "aeroplain: the wind-up bird chronicles," a collection of musical tracks produced in Copenhagen between

December 2001 and January 2003 and "inspired by and created around the book by the Japanese author Haruki Murakami called *The Wind-Up Bird Chronicle*." (On his Web site Massimo explains: "Aeroplain is not a misspelling of the word 'Aeroplane', even though it toys with this very common misspelling. It is a compound of the words 'aero' and 'plain'—a description of the music in more than one way.") Needless to say, I was moved to read in the liner notes, "Biggest thanks to Haruki Murakami for this great novel and to Jay Rubin for his wonderful translation." In other words, the melodies that have been going through my head—simple but stirring melodies, the composition of which had been facilitated in part by my own translation and which had the instantaneous catchiness of a Murakami story—were the result of an amazing international confluence of people and events, at the center of which was Haruki Murakami. If this is globalization, I'm all for it, though it can sometimes result in rather long opening paragraphs.

Even if it was the brainchild of a semi-governmental organization designed to solidify a Japanese author's claim on the Nobel Prize as some of us suspected, the "International Symposium and Workshop: A Wild Haruki Chase" was a wonderful occasion—especially for the participants. This was an unprecedented opportunity to meet fellow translators from all over the world and share ideas and impressions not only during the public events (as evidenced by several publications, in-

cluding this book) but over meals and during walks in the woods near Mt. Fuji. Talk about "confluence": this was it in spades! When, six months later, I found myself in the town of Esrum, Denmark, photographing my wife shelling shrimp with Mette Holm and her beautiful daughter Felicia, I knew that the symposium had borne a special kind of fruit.

The situation is very different from 1968, when Yasunari Kawabata won the Nobel Prize for Literature "for his narrative mastery, which with great sensibility expresses the essence of the Japanese mind." Westerners then were unprepared to see a Japanese writer in any but the most ethnocentric terms. Certainly the blinkers had come off in the West by 1994 when the Nobel went to Kenzaburo Oe, "who with poetic force creates an imagined world, where life and myth condense to form a disconcerting picture of the human predicament today." And by the time the city of Cork and the Munster Literature Centre awarded Murakami the short-story prize in September, globalization was in full swing.

As reported in *The Guardian*, Murakami's winning short-story collection, *Blind Willow, Sleeping Woman,* topped a short list that "spanned three continents. First collections from Irish writer Philip Ó Ceallaigh and American author Rachel Sherman were nominated alongside entries from English writer Rose Tremain, Nepal-born Samrat Upadhyay, and Peter Stamm, a Swiss author who writes in German."

I myself arrived in Cork convinced that Murakami couldn't take the prize because it had been won by a Chinese writer the year before. Assuming that political calculations were going to produce an Irish winner this year, I bought a copy of Philip Ó Ceallaigh's *Notes from a Turkish Whorehouse* to check out the competition. I was impressed by the crystal clarity of the writing and touched by a story that Ó Ceallaigh read to the audience during the festival. Thus, when the name "Haruki Murakami" was announced at the prize ceremony, I was stunned. The press release of the Munster Literature Centre further emphasizes how free the jury's deliberations were from the kind of political or nationalistic considerations I had mistakenly thought would be decisive:

> Murakami was chosen as winner of the largest short story prize in the world by a five-member jury that reflects the international nature of the prize. This jury was chaired by Cork-based writer Tom McCarthy . . . and included Irish writer Claire Keegan, English author Toby Litt, Silke Scheuermann, one of Germany's most significant contemporary poets and fiction authors, and American literature scholar Dr. Maurice A. Lee, director of the International Conference on the Short Story in English.
>
> In a statement about their decision, the jury said, 'This is a truly wonderful collection by a

master craftsman of prose fiction. Murakami
writes with great integrity . . . his writing re-
minds us, ultimately, that the reader comes to
published work in search of magic.'

I heard from two of the jury members afterwards,
separately and without any urging from me, that the
decision had been unanimous, arrived at without ran-
cor or misgivings. The final deliberation was by no
means a breeze, however: the jurors came in with different viewpoints, and all the finalists were strong con-
tenders, but after four-and-a-half hours of deadly serious discussion of the six finalists, all the jurors were
comfortable choosing Murakami as the winner. Art
had been the only consideration.

For me (and for Philip Gabriel, who translated more
than half the stories in the book), it was particularly grat-
ifying that the award specifically recognized the role of
the translator in making fiction from a foreign language
competitive with some of the best English writing. Americans, especially, with their self-centered worldview and
poor training in foreign languages, tend to forget the im-
portance of translation in making literature from other
cultures accessible in English. I remember sitting in the
audience in Chicago during an after-play discussion of
the Steppenwolf Theatre Company's production of *after
the quake* in November 2005 and hearing a member of
the theater staff assure the audience of the fidelity of the
adaptation by noting that "99 percent of the words you

heard were Murakami's." No, in fact less than 1 percent of the *words* the audience heard were Murakami's—specifically, the names of the characters. Everything else they heard had been written by the adapter, Frank Galati, or by me, and both Galati and the audience had to take it on faith that my English was in some way "close" to Murakami's Japanese. Few readers realize how completely they are at the mercy of the translator, especially when the two languages involved are as different as Japanese and English.

I like to compare the role of the translator to that of a pianist. Most of the audience members at a piano recital have no access to the original score and they must depend on the performer to make the work audible to them. Of course, the differences in interpretation by different musicians can be very exciting: you can buy hundreds of recordings of the "Pathétique" and compare differences in emphasis and phrasing from one pianist to the next, forming in your own mind something of an ideal interpretation never quite attained by any one musician. The economics of book publishing make such an opportunity all but impossible in literature, though perhaps that is beginning to happen in the case of the nineteenth-century Russian novelists. It will be a long while before second and third interpretations of Murakami works emerge.

One Murakami novel for which there have been frequent calls for a new—or at least restored—translation is *Nejimakidori kuronikuru* or, as it is known

in my English version, *The Wind-Up Bird Chronicle.* The current editions (US and UK) bear a notification in small type that the book has been "Translated and adapted from the Japanese," with no indication of what that "adaptation" consists of. In fact, as I explained in my book, *Haruki Murakami and the Music of Words* (Vintage UK, 2005), pp. 304–13, the US publisher, Alfred A. Knopf, insisted on a work that was significantly shorter than the original, and I chose to do the cuts myself (with Murakami's help) rather than let a random editor do the job. Since then, I have occasionally suggested to Knopf that the time might be ripe for an uncut edition, but they have shown no interest in the idea.

One question I would have to reconsider for a restored translation would be whether or not to put an "s" at the end of the word "chronicle" in the title. Many people misremember the title of the book even now as *The Wind-Up Bird Chronicles* because the traditional use of "chronicle" in book titles is plural. The Japanese original, *kuronikuru*, sounds singular, but Japanese nouns (even when taken from foreign languages) have no plural form, so one can only be sure from context. One interesting reverse case is Murakami's two books of essays on jazz musicians, *Potoreito in jazu*, which bear the English title *Portrait in Jazz*. In fact, since the books provide literary *portraits* of several jazz musicians, that context makes the word *potoreito*" plural, and the English title should be *Portraits*

in Jazz. When I did my translation of *The Wind-Up Bird Chronicle,* I chose the singular in the title to imply that the novel was a single unified narrative, though in Book 3, chapters 25 and 26 (or, in the uncut original, chapters 27 and 28), where the character Cinnamon offers several "Wind-Up Bird Chronicles" for the protagonist to read, there is good evidence that the plural would be preferable.

I pointed this out to Massimo Fiorentino, who calls his CD *aeroplain: the wind-up bird chronicles,* but he insisted that his use of the plural for his own work was intentional (his notes do in fact refer to my translation with the singular *Chronicle* in the title): he thinks of "each individual melody as one chronicle in itself, thereby using the plural form for the CD. This distinguishes the CD from the book itself while at the same time linking it to the book."

This international consultation on the minutiae of literary interpretation (and the melodies going through my head at the moment) were made possible by the "International Symposium and Workshop: A Wild Haruki Chase" chronicled in this book.

Bellevue, Washington

Haruki Murakami

Au sud de la frontière, à l'ouest du soleil

roman

belfond

South of the Border, West of the Sun, France

Caçando carneiros

Haruki Murakami

A Wild Sheep Chase, Brazil

The Wind-Up Bird Chronicle, Spain

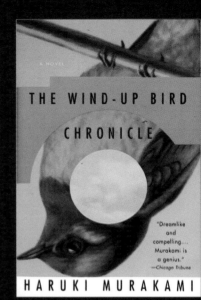

The Wind-Up Bird Chronicle, UK

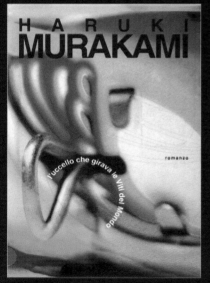

The Wind-Up Bird Chronicle, Italy

The Wind-Up Bird Chronicle,
Romania

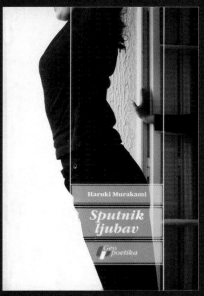

Sputnik Sweetheart, Croatia

Sputnik Sweetheart, Germany

Sputnik Sweetheart, Portugal

Sputnik Sweetheart, Denmark

Харукі
Муракамі

Танцюй,
танцюй,
танцюй

ЛІТЕРАТУРА

Том 1

FOLIO

Dance Dance Dance Ukraine

Kafka on the Shore, Norway

Kafka on the Shore, Taiwan

Kafka on the Shore, China

Norwegian Wood, Indonesia

Norwegian Wood, Spain (Catalan)

The Evening Spidermonkey,
Korea

Харуки

Мураками

Джазовые портреты

To Translate
and to Be Translated
Haruki Murakami

I never reread my own works unless there is some very special reason. It may sound impressive for me to say that I do not look back on my past, but the truth is that I find it a bit embarrassing to take my own novels in my hands, and I know I would not like them anyway if I were to read them. I would rather look forward and think about what I will be doing next.

So it is not unusual for me to completely forget what and how I wrote in my earlier books. Quite often,

when a reader asks me what a particular passage means in a certain work, I wonder if there is such a passage at all. It also sometimes happens that I read something that catches my attention in a book or magazine and think, "This stuff isn't bad at all," only to discover that it is an excerpt of my own writing. As presumptuous as it sounds, that is what happens.

On the other hand, I am quick to recognize my writing when the passage being quoted is one that I do not like. For whatever reason, I can always tell. I tend to forget the good work but remember clearly those places that I am unhappy with. It is a strange thing . . .

Anyhow, typically by the time a novel of mine is published in another language a few years after I have finished writing it, I can no longer remember clearly what I wrote. Of course I never forget the entire plot, but much of the detail will have been wiped clean from my memory—not that I have a very good memory to begin with—just as the moisture from a summer shower on an asphalt road evaporates quickly and soundlessly.

I usually leaf through translations of my novels if they are in English. Once I start reading one, I often find it absorbing (because I have forgotten how it goes) and fly through to the end, thrilled and occasionally moved to laughter. So when a translator asks how the translation is, all I can say is, "Well, I was able to read through it smoothly. Seems good to me." There are hardly any technical comments that I can make—"This part was so-and-so, that part was so-and-so."

Although I am asked what it is like to have my novels translated into other languages, I honestly have little such awareness.

If a translation can be read smoothly and effortlessly, and thus enjoyably, then it does its job as a translation perfectly well—that is my basic stance as the original author. For that is what the stories that I conjure and lay out are really about. What the story says over and beyond that is a question in the realm of the "front room" that awaits after a translation has safely cleared the "front yard" portion of the work, or of the "central room" that lies further on.

For me, one of the joys of my works being transformed into another language is that I can reread them in a new form. By having a work converted into another language by someone else's hand, I can look back and reconsider it from a respectable distance and enjoy it coolly as a quasi-outsider, as it were, whereas I never would have read it again if it had remained only in Japanese. In so doing, I can also reevaluate myself from a different standpoint. That is why I am very thankful for the translators who translate my novels. It is certainly a delight to have my works read by readers in other countries, but at the same time, it is a joy that my works can be read by me myself—though, unfortunately, for now this is limited to English.

Put differently, when a literary world that I have created is transposed into another linguistic system, I feel as if I have been able to dissociate me from my-

self, which gives me a good deal of peace. One may say, then, that I might as well write in a foreign language from the start. But this is not so easily done, for reasons of skill and capability. That may be why, in my own way, I have tried to write my novels using prose that I have constructed by first converting Japanese, my mother tongue, into a mock foreign language in my head—that is, by clearing away the innate everydayness of language that lies in my self-consciousness. Looking back, it seems as if that is what I have always done.

Seen in that light, my process of creative writing may closely correspond to the process of translation—or rather, in some respects they may be two sides of the same coin. I have been translating (from English to Japanese) for many years myself, and I know how hard the job of translation is, as well as how much fun it is. I also understand to some extent how immensely the flavor of the text can vary from one translator to another.

What is most needed for a good translation is probably linguistic skill. But another quality that I think is equally important, especially in the case of fiction, is a love full of personal bias. Put most radically, I would say that is all you need. What I expect above all in translations of my works is just that. A love full of bias is, in the face of this uncertain world, one of the things I adore the most, with a deeply biased love.

Translated from "Honyaku suru koto to, honyaku sareru koto," *Wochi Kochi*, August/September 2006: 8–9. Originally published in the Japanese language in *Kokusai Koryu* 73 (1996).

A Wild Haruki Chase
Reading Murakami Around the World

How to View
the "Haruki Boom"

Inuhiko Yomota

Until the 1980s, Japan was seriously troubled by a gap
between its economic power and its cultural power
in global terms. A frequent argument was that Japanese culture, while refined, has a highly peculiar nature and is unlikely to enjoy international popularity.
These claims were grounded in the assumption that
even though Japan has been an exporter of consumer
electronics—beginning with the transistor radio and
followed by the video cassette recorder, the Walkman,

karaoke, the digital camera, and other products—it lags far behind when it comes to exporting the cultural software that these technologies convey.

From the end of the 1980s onward, though, gradual changes were seen in the situation surrounding Japan's cultural configuration. With the emergence of colossal global media channels, many cultural commodities born in Japan began to make inroads overseas. Today, Japanese subculture is accepted not only by our East Asian neighbors, but by people worldwide, and it is coming to have a decisive impact on the sensibility of a rising generation.

The international "Haruki boom" gained momentum in the 1990s, around the same time as anime (Japanese animation) and Japanese-made computer games pushed into global markets. Unlike the works of his Japanese predecessors, such as Jun'ichiro Tanizaki and Yasunari Kawabata, Murakami's works are not being translated and consumed overseas as those of an author who represents Japanese culture. In every society, his works are first accepted as texts that assuage the political disillusionment, romantic impulses, loneliness, and emptiness of readers. Only later do they fully realize that the author was born in Japan and that the books are actually translations. While it is true that Murakami is a Japanese writer who writes in Japanese, the cultural sensibility that he draws on, the music and films that appear in his works, and the urban way of life that he depicts are all of a nature that cannot be

attributed to any single place or people, drifting and circulating as they do in this globalized world.

Absence of Japanese stereotypes

In South Korea, where anti-Japanese sentiment is historically strong, Murakami's works are enjoyed first and foremost as "Haruki literature" rather than as Japanese literature. If the names of the characters in *Norwegian Wood* were replaced with Danish-sounding or Polish-sounding names, Danish and Polish readers would read the book easily believing it to be a novel of their own country. And so on and so forth.

This aspect of the Haruki boom comes into sharper relief when compared with the *Oshin* television drama series that was broadcast in Japan on NHK television in 1982. The series was subsequently aired in other Asian countries, African countries, and the Soviet Union, where it won huge ratings. This biographical epic about a woman who rises from poverty and finds happiness after many years of hardship plainly depicts the ethos that traditionally guided the Japanese—an ethos that developing countries for a time found necessary for ideological reasons.

Murakami's novels are largely devoid of anything suggestive of this sort of traditional "Japaneseness." It was in the context of their cultural scentlessness, if you will, that his works crossed national boundaries and

gained a strong following overseas. *Norwegian Wood* may feature Beatles nostalgia, but no samurai or geisha appear in it; the novel is notable for its absence of Japanese stereotypes. Thus, around 1990, a shift occurred in the international image of Japanese culture from the *Oshin* model to the Haruki model.

Cultural cosmopolitanism versus locality

The primary aim of the Murakami symposium was neither to honor Murakami as a representative of Japanese literature nor to naïvely celebrate his part in enhancing our national prestige, jumping at the possibility of his winning a Nobel Prize in literature. Although it is important to shed light on the smaller problems that arise in the course of translating between particular languages, a symposium of this kind must not be just an occasion for "Haruki geeks" to narcissistically identify with one another. The true issue lies in the dimension of the translation of cultures.

Japanese culture is likely to continue to overcome national boundaries and be widely accepted overseas. The question is whether this phenomenon is to be openly welcomed if cultural scentlessness is a requisite for winning public popularity in a global age. How far should the geopolitically determined locality of Japanese culture be compromised for it to be understood internationally? The issue of cultural cosmopolitan-

ism versus locality needs to be freshly debated at this juncture.

Translated from "Haruki bomu wo do kanga-eruka," *Wochi Kochi*, August/September 2006: 10–11.

The Global Distributed Self-Mirroring Subterranean Neurological Soul-Sharing Picture Show

Richard Powers

In a laboratory in Parma ten years ago, around the time that Haruki Murakami was writing his masterpiece, *The Wind-Up Bird Chronicle*, a team of international neuroscientists stumbled upon one of the most remarkable discoveries about mental functioning in our lifetime. As often happens, the discovery was a lucky accident. The researchers, under the lead of Giacomo Rizzolatti, were exploring the premotor cortex of ma-

caques—that area of the monkey's brain responsible for moving its muscles. They sunk an electrical probe into the monkey's brain tuned to detect the firing patterns of single neurons.

Rizzolatti's researchers located a neuron in the macaque's brain that gave off a steady signal whenever the monkey reached out to grab an object. When the monkey's arm rested, the neuron fell silent. They had located an individual neuron involved in moving the animal's arm. This surreal scene already presents a Murakamiesque image: a small, defenseless creature wired up to detection devices, a faint signal passing back and forth between the flashing, high-tech outside and the murmuring network within. And the truth that the researchers uncovered could almost be a Murakami theme: in the fantastic landscape of representation, reality begins.

But the neuroscientists were shocked when one of their animals, during a break between experiments, began signaling from its premotor cortex even when its arm was at rest. The monkey's brain was moving *something*, but it wasn't the monkey's muscles.

Even stranger: this stream of motor-neuron activity happened only when the *experimenters themselves* reached out to grab the same objects. Simply watching another creature move somehow triggered internal symbolic movement inside the monkey. The arm in the world and the *idea* of an arm in symbol space were both controlled by the same neurons.

Rizzolatti's crew named their new discovery "mir-

ror neurons. " Here was something never before suspected: Electrical impulses moved muscles, but images of moving muscles also made symbolic muscles move, all on the same strange, tangled loop of mental circuitry.

The report of mirror neurons produced a neuroscience revolution. A part of the brain that did physical things was being cannibalized for making imaginary representations, what Rizzolatti called "motor ideas." These motor ideas underlie our grasp of space, our interpretation of others' actions, and even our semantic categories. Science had laid bare the neurological basis of empathy: brain maps, mapping other brains as they were busy mapping ours.

Experiments soon revealed that humans, too, were crawling with mirror neurons. Mirror-systems grew tendrils, snaking into other higher cognitive processes: speech and learning, facial decoding, threat analysis, the perception of emotions, and the formation of social intelligence. Doing and imagining were not independent processes, but two aspects of the same circuitry. As John Skoyles and Dorian Sagan write in *Up From Dragons: The Evolution of Human Intelligence* (McGraw-Hill, 2002):

> The primary visual cortex takes up more blood when imagining something than when actually seeing it. . . . When we imagine ourselves running . . . our heart rate goes up. In one study, a group of people imagining physical exercises

increased their strength by 22 percent, while those doing the real thing gained only slightly more, by 30 percent. [pp. 36–38]

Now keep this looping, mirroring, collaborative model of the mind in *your* prefrontal cortex as Murakami describes how he conceives of the dream landscapes that fill his novels:

We have rooms in ourselves. Most of them we have not visited yet. . . . From time to time we can find the passage . . . We find strange things . . . old phonographs, pictures, books. . . . They belong to us, but it is the first time we have found them. . . . I think dreams are collective. Some parts do not belong to yourself . . . [Thompson, Matt, "The Elusive Murakami," *The Guardian* (UK), May 26, 2001]

Communal dreams, interior rooms furnished with other people's possessions: this sounds like Jungian collective unconsciousness. And until recently, Jung remained the most sweeping account of how the individual self is stitched together from out of vast, shared spaces and times. Now, in the looping, shared circuitry of mirror neurons, science has hit upon an even richer description of our communal, subterranean truths, the truths that Murakami's mirrorscape of symbols brings into existence as we read him.

41

Murakami's fiction deploys, side by side, as part of one marvelously webbed story, distinct—if multiply connected—independent narrative frames. Some of these story frames could pass for conventional social realism. A contemporary, urban world much like Tokyo, filled with references to mass consumer culture and peopled with wonderfully realized "realistic" characters provides the grounding for the unfolding story. But alongside this story—folded through or *underneath* it—fantastic, chthonic worlds spring up and seep into normal existence, entwining and overpowering realism in their weird tendrils. "There's another world that parallels our own," Oshima assures Kafka in *Kafka on the Shore* (Knopf, 2005), "and to a certain degree you're able to step into that other world and come back safely. As long as you're careful. But go past a certain point and you lose the path out. It's a labyrinth . . . the principle of the labyrinth is inside you" [p. 326].

Such a parallel narrative world occurs in *Hard-Boiled Wonderland and the End of the World*. In one frame, set in an apocalyptic, data-driven Tokyo, the Calcutecs and the Semiotecs fight for possession of the mental encryption keys that give power over runaway data. In the other frame, a character arrives at a walled city surrounded by a forest, to take up residence reading the dreams imprinted in unicorn skulls. These worlds are linked, but how? Do they dream each other into existence? Perhaps the worlds of this magnificently

mirroring book cast each other's shadows inside a recursive cortex.

Murakami's characters, set loose between these intersecting worlds, are forced to embark on detective spelunking. They venture downwards into walled enclaves, climb into deep wells, or drop below the surface of seismically shaken cities, searching for the rules that connect the banal and the fantastic, the material and the mental. They climb up into volcanic craters or hide themselves on Greek islands. Where else can they go but into these subterranean terrains of symbol and surprise? As the neuroscientist Michael Gazzaniga estimates, "Ninety-eight percent of what the brain does is outside of conscious awareness."

Even in Murakami's most realistic narratives, the opening into the underworld is never far away. In *Norwegian Wood* (Vintage International, 2000), Toru Watanabe describes a threatening well that Naoko, the woman he loves, insists lies somewhere nearby, invisible, just off the path that they walk along. Watanabe explains:

I have no idea whether such a well ever existed. It might have been an image or a sign that existed only inside Naoko, like all the other things she used to spin into existence inside her mind in those days. Once she had described it to me, though, I was never able to think of that meadow scene without the well. From that day forward, the image of a thing that I had never laid

eyes on became inseparably fused to the actual
scene of the field that lay before me. I can go so
far as to describe the well in minute detail . . .
It was deep beyond measuring, and crammed
full of darkness, as if all the world's darkness
had been boiled down to their ultimate density.
"It's really, really deep," said Naoko, choosing
her words with care . . . "But no one knows
where it is." [p. 5]

These striking sentences might have come directly
from Rizzolatti's lab in Parma: Naoko's description
triggers Watanabe's mirroring participation. Her imaginary mental icon alters his *actual* meadow. Although
"no one knows" where the well is, the immeasurable
depth and darkness of Naoko's imagination becomes
as palpable to Watanabe as if he himself had fallen
into it. And in a sense, he has, in the world of mental mirrors. As Watanabe later learns, from Naoko's
roommate Reiko, inside the buried confines of Naoko's
sanatorium, "We're all each other's mirrors, and the
doctors are part of us" [p. 97].

One of the great pleasures in reading Murakami
lies in imagining just what links might unfold between
these two worlds of banal realism and underground
phantasmagoria. These worlds obviously hinge on
each other, but the hinge is most often the story process itself. When the factual and the fabulous collide,
we are left wonderfully shattered, waiting to see what

new collages might emerge out of the shards of impact. Murakami has compared his protagonists to video gamers, detached yet engaged, moving through the startling landscape of their lives as through the levels of an open-ended role-playing adventure. We readers too are drawn along, on the far side of another tilted mirror, changed by the changing game, and even helping to alter its outcome.

The 1990s, officially proclaimed the Decade of the Brain, produced numerous discoveries about the brain as strange and marvelous as any Murakami plot. Where once the mind was a unitary thing, subsequently split by Freud and Jung into two or three independent parts, it is now divided into *hundreds* of distributed subsystems, every one of them a discrete, signaling agent inside a loose and tangled confederation.

In place of simple brain hierarchies with one-way flows of control, contemporary neuroscience gives us constellations of areas, each sharing reciprocal relations with many others. Eight mental maps are used to process hearing, and at least twenty-two areas combine to perform vision. Recognizing a face requires the coordination of dozens of networked regions. Even speaking a word is like getting dozens of musicians to perform a symphony. Clearly the self—floating on this jumble of processes—is not an identity, but a noisy parliament, negotiating itself into being, constantly updating and updated by all those other external selves that it brushes up against.

A break in any part of this multiple, multidirectional mental house of mirrors can radically change the selves that we improvise. For example: people who suffer bilateral damage to the anterior cingulate lose their ability to distinguish reality from imagination. They believe that they have actually visited places that they've only heard about, and they think they have really done things that have happened only in dreams. But the new neuroscience also points out that such mental states, resulting from brain damage, may also occur in weaker forms in ordinary consciousness.

Murakami knew all this, well before the Decade of the Brain. Hence his characters who move through a landscape unable to tell whether they are following some external physical rules or are constructing them internally. As Kafka learns at the beginning of *Kafka on the Shore,* "this storm isn't something that blew in from far away, something that has nothing to do with you. This storm is you. Something inside of you" [p. 5]. In the story, "Super-Frog Saves Tokyo" (*after the quake,* Vintage UK, 2003), Frog tells the hospitalized Katagiri about their shared epic underground struggle to save the city from an earthquake which Katagiri cannot now remember: "The whole terrible fight occurred in the area of imagination. That is the precise location of our battlefield. It is there that we experience our victories and our defeats" [p. 98].

In contemporary neuroscience, the boundary between the inner map and outer physical reality results

from tentative and multilateral negotiations, constantly in danger of breaking down. A break between two brain subsystems can upset the entire construction of self, producing a plethora of symptoms which might serve nicely for a Murakami plot. People cease to be able to identify familiar objects. They grow unable to tell whether oranges are smaller or larger than cherries. They lose their ability to distinguish between two faces. They deny that their left arms belong to them. They duplicate physical places, believing that their own, familiar houses are mere copies. They lose the use of concrete words while retaining abstract ones. They think that they are blind when they aren't, or that they can see when they're blind. They believe that their loved ones have been replaced by impostors. They hallucinate cartoon characters in a sea of actual people.

Such states of consciousness sound familiar to any Murakami reader. Think of Miu, stranded on top of the Ferris wheel in *Sputnik Sweetheart* (Vintage International, 2000), staring down on her own apartment and seeing herself making love to a man she abhors. Think of K., the narrator of that book, describing his own depersonalization: "My hand was no longer my hand, my legs no longer my legs . . . someone had rearranged my cells, untied the threads that held my mind together [p. 170]. . . . I can no longer distinguish between one thing and another, between things that existed and things that did not" [p. 205]. Or think of the narrator of *A Wild Sheep Chase* (Kodansha Interna-

tional, 1989): "The more I thought about it, the more that other me became the real me, making this me here not real at all" [p. 245].

Given the endlessly bizarre states of consciousness that neuroscience describes, Murakami's novels—even their strangest of interludes—begin to seem every bit as realistic as those of his beloved Raymond Carver. Perhaps more than any other living writer, Murakami understands the paradox of the modular and distributed brain: Consciousness is only ordinary, only solid, only predictable when you remain unconscious about what it is constantly doing to you. As Toru Okada realizes, down at the bottom of his cavernous well in *The Wind-Up Bird Chronicle* (Vintage International, 2000):

> This person, this self, this me, finally, was made somewhere else. Everything had come from somewhere else, and it would all go somewhere else. I was nothing but a pathway for the person known as me. [p. 262]

Murakami's every sentence knows the world is not as real as it seems, not as simple as our raucous multi-hundred-module brains pretend it to be. And strangest of all, as his stories suggest, may be the brain's willingness to treat just about anything that its own cacophony shouts out as a coherent story. K. and Sumire, the joint tale-spinners of *Sputnik Sweetheart*, work out the truth between them:

A real story requires a kind of magical baptism to link the world on this side with the world on the *other* side [p. 16]. . . . On the flip side of everything we think we absolutely have pegged lurks an equal amount of the *unknown* [p. 134]. . . . Just a single mirror separates us from the other side. [p. 157]

But if his own stories are steeped in the endless weirdness hiding just inside everyday life, how then to account for Murakami's astonishing popularity throughout the world? His works have been translated into three dozen languages. He is a perennial bestseller throughout Europe. He has spawned a generation of imitators around the Pacific Rim. He is the subject of full-length books, countless scholarly articles, and television documentaries. In the United States, he is considered among the few truly important international writers. How can the same writer be a runaway bestseller in Italy and Korea, a cultural phenomenon in Turkey, and the object of highest literary respect in countries as different as Russia and China? One explanation for his astonishing international success may be this deep attunement to the strangeness of the distributed and modular brain—a strangeness not culturally constructed but in itself *the* fundamental transcultural and universalizing condition.

Murakami taps into the international youth culture. His models are American, from Fitzgerald to Da-

vid Lynch. He is hip and accessible and funny, and he loves to refer to objects of global consumer culture recognizable from Dallas to Dacca. As such, his success, at least superficially, resembles the worldwide popular music that his characters so dearly love.

But the breezy style and familiar brand-name references mask something more profound. Much has been made, by critics such as Reiichi Miura, about Murakami's status as a leading practitioner of transnational fiction for a globalizing world. His stories not only grasp the zeitgeist of globalization: they *embody* it. He extends Fitzgerald's Lost Generation and Kerouac's road wanderers into our current moment, where displacement has become universal and our fixed sense of national identity is vanishing.

Like his characters, Murakami is neither wholly Japanese nor wholly Americanized, nor does he advocate for any other group identity. In interviews, the question of nationality seems to fluster Murakami. He is unwilling either to embrace or reject the notion, and sometimes chooses to avoid the question altogether. This ambivalence towards nationality places him among the first truly global writers without fixed abode, free to travel everywhere. Pico Iyer, himself a supremely transnational writer, says:

> Murakami is the first Japanese novelist I know who has been able to straddle East and West. He disarms us by writing as if he were just

down the neighborhood in Madison, Wisconsin, or San Antonio. He calls upon those elements of the global consciousness—pasta, Charles Mingus, Raymond Carver—that seem to float above any particular ground and so speak to Everyplace. [Quoted in Kelts, Roland, "Haruki Murakami vs. the End of the World," *Village Voice*, September 25, 2002]

Murakami's books understand the terrifying disorientation of late, globalizing capitalism and our status as refugees inside it. As much as any contemporary writer, Murakami grasps the bewildering fluidity of commoditized life. All the countries of the earth are now party to that knowledge, and so his books speak to anyone who has felt how easily nationality, self, and all other traditional memberships disappear into the flows of global capital and commerce.

Globalization, in its massive, expanding enterprise, destroys the familiar and local, while rendering bafflement ubiquitous. In the world of high-tech, late capitalism, the banal exists right next to the inconceivable and the miraculous. I do not need to rehearse the miracles for you—the defeats of time and space, the triumphs and transformation and transcendence of the human. The most fantastic development in Murakami is no more strange or estranging than what we live with every day of our lives.

But here is the strange mirror that maps our in-

side with our outside: in its estranging effect upon the individual, globalization surreally resembles those maladies of disrupted consciousness that contemporary neuroscience explains so well with its distributed models. It leaves us defamiliarized, face-blind, doubling ourselves, insisting that our own home is an alien mock-up. Individual identity is under siege, both from above and below. Being driven out of comfortable, coherent national boundaries into the "breathtaking interchangeability" of global markets naturally feels, down at eye level, much like being forced out of the old, single, unitary self into a loose confederation of hundreds of brain regions. In both cases, the integral "I" is left hopelessly fluid, cut adrift and condemned to improvise, driven from an illusory home into deep and subterranean places, alien landscapes where our inner phantasms vibrate freely to the outer movements of others.

And through this alien, fluid, and reformulating place, Murakami's children move, underground, by flashlight, bumping up against the end of one world even while stumbling upon the start of another. Yet strangely and wonderfully—and herein lies the secret of his astounding literary success—Murakami's protagonists respond to the disintegration of old certainties not with terror, but with a widening thrill of discovery. When asked in an interview in the *Guardian* to account for his success with so broad a readership throughout the globe, Murakami suggests that "my books can of-

fer them a sense of freedom—freedom from the real world." Freedom, that is, from the misleading belief that the world offers us a fixed and predictable abode, and liberation from the lie that we are solid, unitary, and unchanging entities.

His fiction embraces the sense that "we" are the product of hundreds of different countries, hundreds of different neuronal regions mocking up a running approximation of self and surroundings. His stories find remarkable comfort in inhabiting a distributed self, a new cosmopolitanism even as old states vanish. Where can we hope to live, in the age of the universal refugee? No place but everywhere. In homelessness is our freedom to inhabit any place in the world, for all places everywhere arise from the mirroring negotiation of mind.

And our reward in reading Murakami is the pleasure of pirating, inside our own cortex, his neural cosmopolitanism. Real or surreal, global or local, familiar or strange: Murakami's fiction knows that all of these worlds are affirmed or rejected entirely inside the theater of the brain. Such an embrace of the ultimate neural nature of all experience might easily collapse into self-absorption, as it threatens to do in the extremes of conventional and postmodern fiction that flank Murakami's work. We would each of us be locked inside a sealed and unknowable simulation of self, were it not for the truth that globalization, neuroscience, and Murakami's fiction have all simultaneously hit upon:

there is no self unto itself. The private life is always a propagating conversation, always a mirroring of something far larger than it can ever formulate.

It comes as no surprise, then, to realize how dominated Murakami's stories are by all the varieties of love: Romantic, platonic, familial, companionable, comic, sexual, nostalgic, kinky, archaic, lonely, selfish, selfless: as many kinds of love as there are brain regions. If his work says yes to the uncanny oddity of existence, certainly the oddest thing it must affirm is the outlandish possibility—no, make that the *outrageous necessity*—of connection. If his work could be said to have one overriding theme, one irresistible attraction, it must be this deep and playful knowledge: No one can tell where "I" leaves off and others begin.

The maze of mind will always stand between us and the real. But the inescapable cavern of the brain leaves a single way out: the empathetic leap, transnational commerce, the mirroring neuron. We can never know the world, but in our shared bewilderment, we *can* know each other. As the schoolteacher writes in *Kafka on the Shore*: "As individuals each of us is extremely isolated, while at the same time we are all linked by a prototypical memory" [p. 210].

Murakami's fiction claims what the enlightened of every era and country have always claimed: existence is fleeting; certainty is illusory; thought is stranger than you can think; reality is a running compromise; the self is a house on fire, so get out while you can. Even where

we have no home to go back to, we might yet inhabit a better place—someplace improvised, provisional, tentative, forever inexplicable. One where the movement of our very muscles—not least of all the heart—where our very movements somehow in fact embody all of the fictional empathetic resonance that our cells perpetually manufacture. A place where seeing and being share the same circuitry. A place infinitely larger than the old small self. Call it the mirroring motor cortex. Call it the core of symbolic connection. Call it that chief of strangenesses, the interlocking dream, the alien reality parallel to, folded through, or *underneath* this world: love. "Love can rebuild the world," Oshima tells Kafka [p. 209]. "So everything's possible when it comes to love."

What We Talk About When We Talk About Murakami

Roland Kelts

Most American readers who like Haruki Murakami's stories do not merely like them. They fall in love. They cling to the meanings they find, they caress the books. They see in Murakami narratives the tones and colors of their own dreams, expressions of something lyrical yet pure, and partly ineffable. Something they know and feel, but maybe cannot explain.

Not all American readers like or love Murakami's art, of course. And those who do not often complain of

the same quality that ultimately seduces his American admirers—or more accurately, his "fans": the ineffable. The inconclusive endings, the disappearing characters, the sometimes bedazzling but forgotten narrative threads, spooling off into a cool oblivion.

I wrote some years ago of the confused reaction to Murakami among American critics. He was being compared to Franz Kafka, though he was significantly warmer and less anxious; to Thomas Pynchon and Don DeLillo, though he was less vaudevillian than the former and less austere than the latter; to Raymond Carver and Raymond Chandler, though those writers shared only first names; and he was even spoken of next to Mishima, with whom Murakami shared nothing more than citizenship.

Since I wrote those words, Murakami has won the award named after his chillier European predecessor, Kafka, often a precursor to the Nobel Prize. He has outpaced his American seniors, Pynchon and DeLillo, in the hip-lit category, retaining his cool intellectualism while reaching younger readers with his romanticism. He has made Carver famous in his native land, and he has returned to Chandler to translate the "Long Goodbye"—amid translating F. Scott Fitzgerald's *The Great Gatsby*, a goal he set for himself twenty-five years ago.

In short: It's no longer worthwhile understanding Murakami via references to his "Western" influences, or to his essential "Japaneseness"—though some Americans continue to try.

John Updike is one of the few American author-intellectuals whose literary criticism often equals if not exceeds his latest fiction. But his attempt at reviewing Murakami's last novel translated into English, *Kafka on the Shore*, was a revealing travesty. In the pages of the *New Yorker* magazine, Updike's longstanding patron, the esteemed American author seemed desperate to account for Murakami's popular and critical success. The novel, he wrote, "is a real page-turner, as well as an insistently metaphysical mind-bender" that "seems more gripping than it has a right to be and less moving, perhaps, than the author wanted it to be."

Strange uncommitted shuffle-step there, on which Updike ends with the following duck into the curtains to slink offstage: "Existence as something half empty—a mere skin on the essential void, a transitory shore—needs, for its celebration, a Japanese spiritual tact."

What does that mean?

One of America's premier novelists and literary critics accounts for the sublime mysteries of a Murakami feast by excusing himself from the table? What is a "Japanese spiritual tact?" And if you need it to celebrate his stories, why is Murakami so popular in America and elsewhere in the world?

Whether *Kafka on the Shore* will emerge as one of Murakami's finest novels or not remains debatable. But Updike's response is more revealing.

Here is a writer (Murakami) whose reputation has earned him a "cool" cachet as a major international

figure on the leading edge of literary fiction, able to integrate laid-back contemporary urban malaise and consumerism with historical horrors, as he does so well in *The Wind-Up Bird Chronicle*, whose stories appear regularly in the *New Yorker* itself—and whose readers treat him like a rock star, lining up several deep at a New York City Barnes and Noble, while he appears nonchalantly amid security guards and wearing thick black sunglasses.

And here is the American novelist and critic (one whom, I must admit here, I admire intensely for his best work, and whose art and criticism continues to serve as a model for me), raised in the American 1950s, brilliant, schooled in Western dualisms: high and low culture, art and pop, Christianity and Paganism, white light and dark evil.

It seems to me that the heart of the dissonance is this: Murakami is neither simply "hot" (warm, passionate, wetly emotional, in Japanese terms) nor "cool" (detached, ironical, systematic). In his best art, he is both, or he is all, or he is neither one.

In researching my new book, *Japanamerica*, about the rising prominence of Japanese artists in the twenty-first century, I asked a producer at the late Osamu Tezuka's production company, Tezuka Productions, what made Tetsuwan Atom (translated as Astro Boy) a truly Japanese character. Walt Disney felt that Mickey Mouse was truly American. Was Atom, his counterpart in Japan, truly Japanese—and why?

"He worries a lot," the producer said. "Japan is the in-between land. Between China and America, between Asia and the West. Our characters inhabit a gray area, and we face a lot of dilemmas."

Fifteen years ago, before the fall of the Soviet Union, before the collapse of the Berlin Wall, and before September 11, 2001, this gray area may have seemed tantalizing, but unreal. Today, the dualisms of Updike's generation, and an America attempting to fight a "war on terror" seem positively antiquated.

Through literature, Murakami's art is at the leading edge of casting such dualisms into their proper historical dustbin. They served their need when there were two "superpowers" roaming our planet. They are now done.

Updike struggles to understand Murakami because Murakami's art does not satisfy a bifurcated view of the world. It inhabits several worlds, as Richard Powers so skillfully noted at the Murakami symposium in Tokyo in 2006, employing neurological advances and analyses to explore Murakami's genius. Our world today is more like a Murakami novel, or an Oshii or Miyazaki anime, or an old *ukiyoe* print, than most Western critics are keen to admit. But the best readers know it.

"Sometimes I think American readers are missing something," Murakami told me in Boston in 2005. "They depend too much on the reviews. But if you can feel the *heat* in a book, that's important. It doesn't have to be perfectly balanced, you know?"

It is difficult to imagine an American critic in any forum praising a literary work for its "heat."

But isn't that what we look for in art? Even the very Bible of American literature, Herman Melville's *Moby Dick*, is virtually nothing without its essential heat, its drive and obsessions.

Still, native emotion can embarrass the natives. Fyodor Dostoevsky is a perfect example: beloved by Western and Asian readers, authors and critics, Dostoevsky is often perceived as an overrated hack at home. Last year, while flying from Boston to New York, I asked my seatmates, two Russians, what they thought of Dostoevsky. They fairly snickered.

"You love him, of course, don't you?" one said, nearly winking. At home in Russia, Dostoevsky is largely considered an overripe embarrassment, a confessional writer, and a man who could not contain himself, whose art is "messy," or, in Murakami's words, overflowing with "heat."

Similarly, most Japanese literati consider Murakami a lightweight, despite his many accolades, a commercial writer who satisfies mass audiences—and has somehow extended his reach to America and beyond.

That is a mistake.

I am neither old enough nor dead enough to argue for Murakami's art as a posthumous etching in the Parthenon of literature. But his art has brought some balance into the American literary world. He is neither purely hot nor purely cold. He is neither purely popu-

lar nor purely literary. American readers fall in love with his stories because he cares about his characters. American critics appreciate and honor his intelligence and diligence. And while he spends a good deal of time thinking about America, he no longer needs it. Nor do the rest of us.

The twenty-first Japanese literary influence Murakami represents is more like a möbius strip: Murakami was heavily influenced by American authors and has been returning the favor in feverish time. Updike's misunderstandings, via a review which was carefully calibrated not to offend suggests that America and its artists may no longer lead the way toward our global literary future. Japan and its artists might.

Japan, partly because of its long history as an in-between nation, is perfectly suited for a wired future, a future of kaleidoscopic possibility and range. And Haruki Murakami, born in Kyoto, raised in Kobe, groomed in Tokyo, and a resident of both Europe and America in his fifty-nine years, was sure of this very early in his career.

Three years ago, Murakami told me a story. He had just opted out of his generation's salaryman rat race at the start of the 1970s. Instead, he took a loan from his wife's family to open a jazz club in Tokyo.

The going got tough, then even tougher. And one night, in dire straits, he and his young wife went walking, trying to sort out how they could pay off an outstanding debt of 30,000 yen/300 dollars.

"Suddenly, we paused. We were both really depressed. But there, on the ground, was an envelope. Three 10,000 yen notes were inside. We held each other, and we started crying. We had no idea how we'd get through the future, but we could get through tomorrow."

Was that true? I asked him.

"It's the *truth*," he said.

This article originally appeared in *Wochi Kochi*, August/September 2006: 8–9.

The Sense of Loss in Murakami's Works and Korea's 386 Generation

Kim Choon Mie

While Haruki Murakami has a wide readership in many countries around the world, it is highly unusual for a Japanese author to enjoy the eager following of hundreds of thousands of South Korean readers. The first work by Murakami to have been introduced in South Korea was *Norwegian Wood*, which was published in Korean in 1989. Until then, Japanese literature was hardly available in South Korea aside from a few short stories by such major authors as Yasunari Kawabata,

Jun'ichiro Tanizaki, and Yukio Mishima that were included in anthologies of world literature and the like. Nobel literature laureates Kawabata and Kenzaburo Oe were unable to win popular support. Ayako Miura was an exception, as all of her works have been translated and widely read, but I suspect that she was in demand partly as a Christian novelist.

The works of these authors, however, were always seen as "literature from Japan." It was with Haruki Murakami that Japanese literature for the first time was accepted by South Korean readers as literature per se without regard to its country of origin.

All of Murakami's works since *Norwegian Wood*—including *A Wild Sheep Chase*, *Dance Dance Dance*, *Kafka on the Shore*, and *After Dark*—have been published in Korean translation and become bestsellers. Notably, *Norwegian Wood* has remained within the top ten in book sales ever since it was published nearly two decades ago. Murakami is the first Japanese author to enjoy such immense popularity in South Korea. In addition to his novels his collections of essays, such as *Yagate kanashiki gaikokugo* [The Sorrows of a Foreign Language], and his photo books, such as *Toi taiko* [Distant Drums], are also popular.

There are over forty South Korean fan sites on the Internet dedicated to Haruki Murakami, and a Web search on his name yields a profusion of Korean Web sites offering commentary on his works and other information relating to the author. The Korean transla-

tion of *Murakami Reshipi* [Murakami Recipes], a recipe book of dishes that appear in Murakami's novels, was published in 2003, and one Web site allows visitors to listen to musical compositions featured in his works. The members of an online forum of Murakami fans (http://cafe.daum.net/harukimake), meanwhile, number over four thousand. That there exist fan sites with thousands of members is proof of the magnetism of Murakami's literary world.

In the melancholy after the end of the student protests

Why are Murakami's works so widely read in South Korea? It is easy to understand why his novels, depicting as they do the sense of failure and loss that Japanese youths experienced in the wake of the widespread radical student movements of the 1960s and the psychological conflict that they subsequently must have experienced in the transition to consumer capitalism, were eagerly accepted in South Korea around 1989. Korean youths who were born in the 1960s and committed themselves to student protests in the 1980s—protests that in Japan were regarded as successful—were stricken with a sense of lethargy and emptiness after having realized a regime change (a direct presidential election was held following the 1987 declaration of democratization that resulted from the upsurge of student protests). Murakami's works perfectly echoed the an-

guish of these youths, the loss of ideology in the course of late capitalist society's shift away from politics and history, the appetite for consumption that filled the void, and the ambience of a vain, if affluent, society.

Thus, the core of Murakami fans in the 1990s consisted of the "386 generation": those who were born in the 1960s, were students in the 1980s, and were in their thirties at the time. The South Korean readership has the distinctive characteristic of largely comprising men, possibly because many male members of the generation, who are now in their late thirties and early forties, are self-proclaimed Murakami freaks even today.

A new generation of authors are emerging from among these readers of Murakami. The impact of Murakami's works on young South Korean writers born between 1960 and 1970 was so great that his writings are considered to be an essential subject in the study of South Korean literature of the 1990s. The styles and expressive techniques of these writers have given rise to a plagiarism debate, attesting to the magnitude of Murakami's influence. They themselves openly admit that they are Murakami freaks who have been greatly influenced by the author's works. Many of them became Murakami fans after reading his works in their twenties, when they were able to share in Murakami's own sense of loss.

The Murakami boom eventually spread to middle and high school students, and *Norwegian Wood* remains a must-read for university students today. It seems

that middle and high school students and university students, each in their own way, feel a sense of fellowship, solidarity, and empathy—of breathing the same air and living in the same age. As some freshmen told me, upon entering university they were told to read Murakami's *Norwegian Wood* and J. D. Salinger's *The Catcher in the Rye*, which they did. It is insightful that eighteen and nineteen year olds, long after even the sense of failure and loss stemming from the dismantling of ideology have been forgotten, continue to look to *Norwegian Wood* and *The Catcher in the Rye* as must-reads.

Perhaps because of the generational difference, younger readers are divided in their impressions of *Norwegian Wood*, unlike the ardent devotees of the 386 generation. Some students say they did not enjoy the book at all, that they thought it was an obscene novel, while others liked it and went on to read other works by Murakami, gradually becoming Murakami freaks.

The socially established acceptance of Murakami

It came as a sort of shock that a paper expressing concern over the fact that Murakami's works have become bibles for South Korean students was recently presented at a seminar that the the Korean Culture and Arts Foundation held on May 25, 2006. The paper was written by Yu Jongho, former professor of English at Ewha Women's University and currently chair profes-

sor at the Korean Language Institute at Yonsei University. In the presentation, titled "The Fall of Literature: A Look at the Murakami Phenomenon," Professor Yu cited the scene in *Norwegian Wood* in which the first-person narrator is reading Thomas Mann's *The Magic Mountain* and pointed out that *The Magic Mountain*, which deeply contemplates all aspects of life, and *Norwegian Wood* stand in stark contrast to one another. He then continued,

> Youth for many is a time in which they experience frustration, a season of anxiety and wandering and of an uncertain future. This book offers a quick and short-lived drug-like relief to these delicate youths who are exhibiting mild depressive symptoms in their season of anxiety. The idea that we are equal in the face of death, failure, and emptiness would be a comfort to anyone. . . . I would not think it problematic if Murakami's novels were cited as mere instances among a vast list of books. What worries me is that many students give his novels as the book that moved or entertained them the most. . . . Readers who are fascinated by *Norwegian Wood* are bound to end up never reading the book *The Magic Mountain* that the protagonist is reading.

The paper is reminiscent of the belles-lettres debate

that was all the rage for a time. But what interests me is not so much the question of what to make of the argument as the very fact that a learned scholar at the apex of South Korean wisdom was compelled to address the phenomenon of the Murakami boom at such a dignified place as the Korean Culture and Arts Foundation. It eloquently demonstrates that the popularity of Murakami has taken root in South Korea as a social phenomenon.

A new literature of the advanced capitalist world

Inuhiko Yomota's keyword of *scentlessness*—the absence of impressions of a specific country—may be insufficient in explaining the acceptance of Murakami beyond generational differences.[*] While Murakami's works are founded on an attitude of criticism toward a consumerist culture, the criticism is expressed not in the form of painful screams but in an ever-cool manner. Coupled with the effect of the sense of loss that imbues his works, I believe that his literature, which seeks ways to live in the capitalist society of the here and now rather than turning its back on reality, has offered a revelation to young South Koreans. It may be said that they have found in Murakami a cultural code with which they can share their own conflicts and woes, a code that perfectly speaks for them.

---

[*]See p. 35.

As the literary critic Chang Sukjuhas remarked, Murakami's works are an icon and code of a new literature that has emerged in the advanced capitalist world of today as it hurtles away from the group to the individual, from ideology to desire, amid the demise of absolute values such as history, divinity, and ideology. Murakami's sensitivity, furthermore, is shared by today's young South Koreans. Employing universal cultural commodities, his works depict not a reality specific to Japan but the urban life of late capitalist society. As such, the more the world grows into a late capitalist society, his novels can be expected to spread with increasing force as transnational cultural commodities.

"From the 1970s onward I lived in a state of spiritual rootlessness," Haruki Murakami said in an interview with the South Korean daily *JoongAng Ilbo* dated September 19, 1995. "I feel that from now on I must create something new," he continued, and commented on the issues of history and morality. Sympathizing as they do with history and morality, two themes universal to humankind, Murakami's novels will likely attract even greater worldwide attention in the coming years. The reason why Murakami's predecessors were translated but were not as widely loved as he is may be because they were unable to present universal themes in a form that can be understood by people across the world. This also seems to have bearings on the discrepancy in how some Japanese authors are regarded in Japan and overseas.

What Russians See in Murakami

Ivan Sergeevich Logatchov

In this article, I would like to consider how Haruki Murakami is received in Russia today and what lies behind his current fame. The "Murakami boom" reached Russian shores some twenty years behind Japan, where he rose to prominence in the 1980s, and spawned many fans of his works. At the time of his emergence in Japan, there were numerous other rising writers. In Russia, however, no contemporary Japanese writers were known when Dmitry Kovalenin's transla-

tion of *A Wild Sheep Chase* ignited Murakami's popularity. Thus, Murakami has become the yardstick by which other contemporary Japanese writers are measured in Russia. At least, the works of Ryu Murakami and Banana Yoshimoto, the next Japanese writers to be translated into Russian, have invariably been compared with Haruki Murakami's works.

To the Japanese, Murakami is but one of many popular writers. In the eyes of the Russians, however, he both symbolizes contemporary Japan and epitomizes the Japanese mentality. Here, I believe, lies a fundamental difference in how his works are received in Japan and in Russia.

The two Murakamis in Russian eyes

There are two well-known Murakamis in contemporary Japanese literature. Though their surnames are the same, Haruki Murakami and Ryu Murakami have highly contrasting lifestyles and little in common as writers. And yet, being familiar with the surname, Russian readers are quick to pick out a Murakami from among the exotic names of Japanese writers.

Needless to say, Haruki Murakami and Ryu Murakami are received in distinct ways. Unlike the works of Haruki Murakami, those of Ryu Murakami are replete with features that hardly suit the taste of Europeans, such as the violence and explicit sexuality of his *Almost*

Transparent Blue. The characters in Ryu Murakami's novels take heroin and have sex after drinking whiskey. After reading all the details of the protagonist's decadent life, readers may be left with such a sense of filth that they feel the urge to wash their hands.

Above all, Russian readers seek the sort of exoticism that they find in Haruki Murakami's works. They are rather disappointed when they have finished reading a Ryu Murakami novel, therefore, not finding it entertaining at all. While Ryu Murakami's works are far from primitive or banal, they are less accessible to Russians than those of Haruki Murakami.

Russian empathy with the protagonist's self-awareness and loneliness

The protagonist's self-awareness, and his loneliness arising from social alienation, an issue frequently addressed by Haruki Murakami, is one that is vitally important and familiar to Russian society today. Following the fall of the Soviet Union many Russians ran up against a similar problem, which might be phrased as, "How should I define my place in the society of the new Russia?" or, "Am I a Russian, or am I a Soviet?" Because life in Russia has lately become insecure and precarious, just as in Murakami's world, Russian readers may be able to discover their own identity and resolve problems involving personal relationships by

reading Murakami's works. His protagonists, who embody contemporary society, offer answers to a variety of compelling questions, such as what human beings are about and what we are living for.

The anecdotes about Russia and Russians that often appear in Murakami's works are also very interesting to Russian readers. Some examples are the nonsense about Leon Trotsky in *Pinball, 1973* and the references to the Nomonhan Incident in *The Wind-Up Bird Chronicle*. These descriptions give Russian readers a good idea of how the Japanese envision Russians.

Acceptance as a modern writer by young Russians

Many Russian readers look upon Murakami as a sophisticated modernist writer. In fact, the very act of reading his works may be taking on the overtones of a fashion rather than a personal pursuit. It has recently become quite common to see someone reading a Murakami book in the Moscow subway. Typically, thinking it is stylish to be reading Murakami, the individual is reading the book without a protective cover, so as to draw the attention of those in the same car to its identity, and wearing a smug look as if to say, "I'm sure you all know exactly what I'm reading." We appear to be seeing the emergence of a new generation of Russians who try to assert that they are different from everyone else by reading books of the moment.

The vast majority of Murakami fans in Russia are either university students or people in their twenties and thirties employed in the financial and media industries. They represent a generation of people who have been groping for their place and a set of values to live by in a changing society. Perhaps they see a reflection of their own vacillation in Murakami's cool and eccentric characters, who distance themselves from those around them. Moreover, his works are exciting and straightforward, and the stories are intriguing. Thanks to a steady stream of translations of works by such contemporary Japanese writers as Haruki Murakami and Ryu Murakami, Russian perceptions of Japan and the Japanese are likely to change substantially.

Speedy translations into Russian

Russian publishers are rushing to translate the works of Haruki Murakami. Three new translations of his works, including the masterpiece *Portrait in Jazz*, were issued in Russia in 2005. Russian readers are already enjoying *After Dark*, while readers in the United States are still working on *Kafka on the Shore*.* The largest bookstores in Moscow, such as Biblio-Globus and Dom Knigi, not only offer large selections of Mura-

---

After Dark was first released in the United States by Knopf in May 2007.

kami's books but have special sections set aside for them. The interest in his works is so high that even major publishers cannot keep up with the demand, and new works often sell out almost as soon as they arrive on store shelves.

Eksmo Press, one of Russia's leading publishing houses, obtained the translation and publication rights for all of Murakami's works in 2005 with a view to publishing a complete collection by the end of 2006. Meanwhile, the second printing of the Russian translation of *Kafka on the Shore*, which was published in December 2004, is almost sold out. *Kafka on the Shore* is the first major novel by Murakami to be translated into Russian before English.

Gripping descriptions of Japanese society

Below I will focus primarily on *The Wind-Up Bird Chronicle* to discuss my observations regarding Murakami's writing style. I believe that his works cannot easily be classified into a single genre. They are not suspense or horror stories along the lines of those of Stephen King, nor are they science fiction or fantasy. But there are views to the contrary, such as that offered by the critic Tetsuya Hatori. In an essay titled "The Modern Significance of Supernatural Powers (An Analysis of *The Wind-Up Bird Chronicle*)," published in the periodical *Kokubungaku* in 1995, Hatori wrote

that *A Wild Sheep Chase*, with its numerous aspects of mysticism and occult horror, is "the Japanese version of the American horror film *The Exorcist*." Murakami can be said to have been greatly influenced by famous Western writers of the twentieth century. His characters drink Heineken instead of sake and eat hamburgers instead of sushi, and this sort of un-Japanese lifestyle arouses the interest and curiosity of overseas readers.

As readers of Murakami are aware, most of his finer novels are in the first person. In this way he imbues readers with his distinctive manner of thinking and draws them deeper into his fantastical universe. Murakami's works have a certain appeal to Russian readers simply by virtue of the abundance of scenes that bear no resemblance to Russian life. Moreover, contemporary Japanese society—the setting of many Murakami novels—is a world apart to the ordinary Russian.

A hard-boiled world of pop culture

Murakami's hard-boiled literature, overflowing with references to pop culture based on the American lifestyle, unfolds like a puzzle and draws readers into a postmodern world in a fantasy-like manner. The excitement is akin to that of a mystery novel. This aspect of his works, along with a literary style reminiscent of improvisational jazz, seems to account in part for his immense popularity.

Lately, Murakami has often been compared with such postmodernist authors as Jack Kerouac and Umberto Eco. *A Wild Sheep Chase* and *Hard-Boiled Wonderland and the End of the World* are said to show the strong influence of Kurt Vonnegut, Jr., while Franz Kafka appears to have influenced *The Wind-Up Bird Chronicle*. Murakami himself has been ambiguous at best when it comes to assessing literary influences on his career.

The critic Koichiro Koizumi compared Toru Okada, the protagonist of *The Wind-Up Bird Chronicle*, with the protagonist of Kobo Abe's *Woman in the Dunes* in his essay "Haruki Murakami's Style: With a Focus on *The Wind-Up Bird Chronicle*," published in *Kokubungaku* in 1995. Murakami himself has admitted that he has been strongly influenced by Kobo Abe, but he also often remarks that he loves the writing style of Fyodor Dostoevsky. In one interview, for instance, he referred to Dostoevsky's *Brothers Karamazov* as "an admirable, ideal novel."

Incidentally, *The Wind-Up Bird Chronicle* contains surprisingly few references to American culture, in contrast to Murakami's earlier novels. A comparison of the novel's first chapter, "Tuesday's Wind-Up Bird: Six Fingers and Four Breasts," with the short story "The Wind-Up Bird and Tuesday's Women," on which the novel is based, illustrates this point well. The protagonist in "The Wind-Up Bird and Tuesday's Women" reads Len Deighton (a British-born author known pri-

marily for spy novels), listens to Robert Plant (former lead singer of Led Zeppelin and a rock vocalist), and eats McDonald's cheeseburgers. Toru Okada of *The Wind-Up Bird Chronicle* listens to Rossini instead of Plant and cooks spaghetti instead of eating cheeseburgers. Although spaghetti could conceivably be likened to fast food like McDonald's hamburgers, Rossini bears no comparison to Led Zeppelin.

A blending of genres

Murakami typically blends several genres in a novel, adopting a flexible literary form spanning various categories that does not adhere to a single genre. *The Wind-Up Bird Chronicle*, for example, crosses over several genres. Aspects of domestic drama, postmodern utopianism, and historical fiction all coexist in the novel.

The domestic-drama part of the book centers on the life of Toru and Kumiko Okada. The opening chapters feature episodes involving their family life, and references are made to the background of their marriage and to the Watayas, Kumiko's eccentric relatives. As the reader approaches part two of the book, however, scenes of everyday life recede and supernatural phenomena come to the fore, as if a dissociation of consciousness or a shift to a different dimension (the otherworld) were taking place. Thanks to Murakami's

use of diverse artistic techniques, the labyrinthine plot is able to segue smoothly from the real world to the otherworld. The author lets his characters wander between reality and fantasy, organizing reality as he pleases. The wall separating reality from pseudo-reality gradually fades away, and the notion of the "here" loses its former meaning. In other words, the "here" simultaneously becomes the otherworld and the real world.

The very title of the novel and the names of its characters—the sisters Malta and Creta Kano, Nutmeg, Boris the Manskinner—have a postmodern feel. *The Wind-Up Bird Chronicle* can also be defined as a postmodern work by the coexistence of the surreal scenes that inundate the novel and true-to-life scenes, most of which depict the Nomonhan Incident and the Sino-Japanese War. With *The Wind-Up Bird Chronicle*, Murakami can be said to have combined for the first time the style of a historical novel with a fantastical postmodern utopianism.

Lu Xun and Murakami: A Genealogy of the Ah Q Image in East Asian Literature

Shozo Fujii

There are strong genealogical ties between the literary works of Lu Xun (1881–1936), the father of contemporary Chinese literature, and Haruki Murakami, both of whom have played critical roles in shaping the closely interrelated identities of nation, citizen, and region in twentieth-century East Asia. The Ah Q image shared by both authors was born in 1921 in Beijing's new literary circle, which was in the process of conceptualizing the nation-state community,

and was inherited by 1980s Tokyo, when the city's literary institutions were reaching a turning point at the door to postmodernism. Lu Xun created the image of the day-laboring peasant Ah Q at the dawn of the new literature movement in China. Haruki Murakami (1949–) then reproduced this image soon after his literary debut in the form of the middle-class figure Mr. Q, who is depicted as a consumable in a democratic state.

Lu Xun and China in the era of the Chinese Revolution

A 200-kilometer train ride southwest from Shanghai brings one to Hangzhou. There the railway turns southeast, and sixty kilometers further on is the ancient city of Shaoxing. Lu Xun was born here as the eldest son of a landowning family. His grandfather was a senior government official who had passed the final level of the Imperial Examinations. By the end of the nineteenth century, however, a string of misfortunes had brought about a swift downfall of Lu Xun's clan. Lu Xun refused to take the Imperial Examinations and chose instead to study in Japan, where he stayed for seven years, beginning in 1902. In Tokyo he encountered what was the most Europeanized urban culture in East Asia at the time.[1]

Punctuated by the Russo-Japanese War (1904–5),

Lu Xun's years in Tokyo came at a time when Japan was forming its backbone as a modern nation-state and Tokyo was undergoing dramatic changes as the capital of a rising empire. Revolutionary progress in transportation and communications had largely homogenized time and space in Japan, and information was coming to reach all corners of the country within a short time. With rapid developments in the education system and print media, information communication had become a booming business.

In 1872 the Meiji government announced the Education Order to establish a national education system. The elementary school enrollment rate was 92 percent by the time Lu Xun arrived in Japan in 1902 and had reached 98 percent by the time of his departure in 1909. In China, statistics in 1919 indicated an attendance rate of no more than 11 percent. In 1909 Tokyo, the dailies *Hochi Shimbun* and *Yorozu Choho* boasted circulations of 300,000 and 200,000, respectively, whereas those of Beijing newspapers were limited to between several hundred and several thousand, according to a 1914 survey. Even Shanghai's *Xinwenbao* and *Shenbao* had circulations of only 20,000 and 15,000. Lu Xun must have felt dizzied by Tokyo, the capital of print media.

Upon returning to China, Lu Xun took up teaching in his native province. In 1912, the year after the Chinese Revolution, he moved to Nanjing to become a manager-level official of the Ministry of Education at

the invitation of Cai Yuanpei, the education minister of the Republic of China's provisional government. He followed the provisional government to Beijing in May of that year.

With Yuan Shikai's failed attempt at an imperial restoration in 1916, the ROC plunged into a decade of military factionalism. Amid all this, the cultural citadel Beijing—home to Beijing University and other universities and technical colleges—became the land of hope for Chinese youths. In 1919 Beijing students led the May Fourth Movement, a nationalistic movement charged with anti-Japanese sentiments.

The modern Chinese literature that burgeoned around this time is otherwise known as May Fourth New Literature. As for Lu Xun, he prolifically published splendid collections of stories after emerging on Beijing's new literary scene with the sensational short story "A Madman's Diary" ["Kuangren riji"]. Many of his works are set in his hometown of Shaoxing, including "My Old Home" ["Guxiang"], in which the first-person protagonist reflects on despair and hope as he returns to his native town for the first time in twenty years to help vacate his family's old worn-down home and reunites with his childhood friend, a tenant farmer who has been diminished to a basket case by the poverty wrought by war and heavy taxes.

"The True Story of Ah Q" ["A Q Zhengzhuan"], released in 1922, is another novella set in a village presumably in the vicinity of Shaoxing. In it, Ah Q, whose

exact name cannot be ascertained, is a day laborer in a village called Weizhuang. He is constantly bullied and ridiculed by his fellow villagers, but he contents himself with distorted logic, calling himself the "number one self-belittler." When he finds himself jobless in the village after making a move on a maid working for the Zhao family in the desire to have a son, Ah Q sets off to the district capital. He eventually returns with money he earned as a bandit and briefly enjoys a better-off life, but he is soon mocked by the villagers again as they learn that he had been no more than a petty assistant to the bandits. Ah Q later dreams of becoming a revolutionary, seeing the local landlords losing their heads over rumors of the Chinese Revolution. His ambitions are thwarted, however, when a young man who had studied in Japan swiftly organizes a revolutionary party in Weizhuang with others. In time, Ah Q is arrested and taken to court as the culprit of a burglary at the home of the Zhao family. He is shot to death before he knows what is happening to him, while the villagers look on with amusement.

With great pathos, Lu Xun depicted Ah Q's technique of psychological victory—that of complacently transferring one's humiliation and defeat to somebody weaker than oneself. By doing so, Lu Xun may be said to have criticized the national character of the Chinese and laid out a theory of the state, purporting that no revolution can be achieved if the people at the grass roots do not change. What Lu Xun portrayed

in Ah Q with fierce criticism and deep sympathy was the national trait of a developing nation-state, and this included not only the lowly peasants who comprised the majority of the Chinese population at the time but also the residents of Beijing and other cities that were in the process of Europeanizing, as well as people like Lu Xun himself.

Delving into the depths of Chinese folklore and religion, Professor Tsuneki Maruo has observed that Lu Xun, while struggling with the inner *gui* (ghost), deftly borrowed from the traditional image of *gui* to sculpt such lonely and friendless figures as Ah Q and Kong Yiji. Maruo then went on to point out that the Q of Ah Q is linked with *gui*, which means "phantom" in Chinese.

The French writer Romain Rolland, it is said, was moved to tears when he read "The True Story of Ah Q" in 1926. The ghost of Ah Q appears to have had a profound influence on a teenage Haruki Murakami as well.

High economic growth in Japan and Murakami's memories of history

Born in 1949, Haruki Murakami moved away from his native Kobe-Ashiya area at the end of the 1960s and studied drama at Waseda University in Tokyo. He launched his literary career in 1979 with the novel

Hear the Wind Sing and followed with more works, including 1982's *A Wild Sheep Chase* and 1987's *Norwegian Wood*, which had sold 8.56 million copies by August 2006.[2] His popularity has been coined the "Haruki Murakami phenomenon." Murakami has continued to write prolifically, presenting *Kafka on the Shore* in 2003 and *After Dark* in 2004, among other works. Today he is one of the foremost authors in contemporary Japanese literature.

Murakami was first translated into Chinese in 1985 in the August issue of the Taipei journal *Xin shu yue kan*. This was also the world's first translation of Murakami. Four major principles exert an effect on the Murakami phenomenon in the Chinese-speaking world, which encompasses mainland China, Hong Kong, and Taiwan. Acceptance of Murakami has spread clockwise from Taiwan to Hong Kong to Shanghai to Beijing, and in each area it has coincided with an approximate halving of the rapid economic growth rate. I call these two features the clockwise principle and the economic leveling-off principle.

The third is what I have termed the post-democratic-movement principle. The democratic movements in Taiwan and mainland China brought about contrasting consequences: In Taiwan, the movement that arose in the late 1980s led to democratization through bloodless reform, but mainland China lost hope for democratization with the tragic Tiananmen Square Massacre of June 4, 1989. These democratic movements

have strongly affected Murakami's acceptance in each area, if with some differences in extent.

The final principle is the *Wood*-high *Sheep*-low principle, which is derived from the fact that in East Asia, including South Korea, interest in *A Wild Sheep Chase* has been relatively low and translations of the novel have been slow coming, whereas *Norwegian Wood* has been well received and swiftly translated. Interestingly, the reverse principle of *Sheep*-high, *Wood*-low, is at work in North America, Europe, and Russia.

Reflections of China and influences of Lu Xun in Murakami's works

Meanwhile, there is clear and consistent evidence of Chinese influences on Murakami's works from early on, as seen in *Hear the Wind Sing* and "A Slow Boat to China" ["Chugoku iki no suro boto"]. In 1998, Murakami told a Tokyo correspondent of a Taiwan newspaper, "My father was drafted and went to mainland China during World War II. . . . All I'm doing is writing the shadows of my memory. To me, China isn't something I struggle to imagine in order to write about; China is an important 'code' in my own life." The shadows of his memory would appear to be his memory of history as formed in his mind by inheriting stories of his father's experiences of the Sino-Japanese

War. "The Sino-Japanese War, or the war that Japan waged in East Asia, has become a key theme for me," Murakami said in an interview with the *Asahi Shimbun* in October 2005.[3]

Murakami's works are tinged not only with images of China but with influences of Lu Xun's writings as well. Murakami opens his first work, *Hear the Wind Sing*, with the following words: "There's no such thing as perfect writing. Just like there's no such thing as perfect despair."[4] These words seem to bear a spiritual resemblance to the words, "Despair, like hope, is but vanity," which appears in the prose poem "Hope" that Lu Xun wrote on January 1, 1925. When Murakami's colloquial words are rephrased in Chinese classic style as, "Writing, like despair, is but imperfection," it is as if Murakami is speaking in Lu Xun's logic of hope.

Murakami also writes in the first pages of *Hear the Wind Sing*, "Still it's awfully hard to tell things honestly. The more honest I try to be, the more the right words recede into the darkness" [p. 6]. Meanwhile, Lu Xun states in his foreword to *Ye Cao* [*Wild Grass*] (Beijing: Foreign Languages Press, 1976), the collection of prose poems in which "Hope" is included, "When I am silent, I feel replete; as I open my mouth to speak, I am conscious of emptiness" [p. 3]. Murakami seems to empathize with Lu Xun's discomfort with the vanity of words.

Lu Xun, in fact, was one of Murakami's favorite authors. William Tay, a comparative literature scholar

from Hong Kong, interviewed Murakami in a "small town in the eastern United States" in November 1992. "It's a long time ago that I used to say I don't read Japanese literature or that I don't want to read it," Murakami told Tay. "I began avidly reading Japanese novels in my forties. . . . As for older authors I've read Soseki Natsume, and also Jun'ichiro Tanizaki. . . . [Among contemporary authors] I would give Kenzaburo Oe. I deeply respect him. . . . And then there was Kobo Abe too." He then replied in response to a question about Chinese literature, "I've only read a few works, mostly classic masterpieces. There's no pattern to it. . . . The novelist I remember now is Lu Xun."[5]

Murakami has also written in regard to his readings, "Back then [in the first half of the 1960s] my family would have a bookstore deliver to us one volume each of Kawade Shobo's *Sekai bungaku zenshu* [Anthology of World Literature] and Chuo Koron Sha's *Sekai no rekishi* [History of the World] every month, and I spent my teenage years reading them volume by volume."[6] Volume forty-seven of the world literature anthology consists of Lu Xun's representative works, including "A Madman's Diary," "My Old Home," and "Tengye Xiansheng" ["Professor Fujino"], along with "The True Story of Ah Q" and *Wild Grass*. It is highly likely that Murakami had read "Ah Q" and *Wild Grass* in the anthology as a teenager.

Lu Xun's Ah Q and Murakami's Mr. Q

About twenty years later, in December 1982, Murakami introduced the character Mr. Q in a short story, "The Kingdom That Went to Ruin" ["Dame ni natta okoku"]. According to the first-person protagonist, his old friend Mr. Q was "my age and about 570 times more handsome than me. He had a fine personality . . . a fine upbringing. . . . His taste in clothes was excellent. He also was an athlete . . . played the piano quite well . . . occasionally read Kenzaburo Oe . . . [and] had a proper, good-looking girlfriend." This would make him a typical middle-class youth. "In a word, Mr. Q was without a fault." Mr. Q is the exact antithesis of the highly defective Ah Q.

The narrator moves away in his fourth year of college and parts with his next-door neighbor Mr. Q. Ten years later, the two happen to sit next to each other at a hotel poolside, but Mr. Q does not notice him. By then, Mr. Q is "something like a director" at a TV station. He engages in a "never-ending" conversation with "a somewhat famous singer or actress" to get her to leave a TV show, and soon the woman throws a large-size Coke at him, some of the contents of which spill on the narrator. Mr. Q politely apologizes and leaves with "a smile just as pleasant in the old days" after having received a warm pardon. He does not recognize his old friend to the very end.

Murakami concludes this tale of reunion

reminiscent of Lu Xun's "My Old Home" with the following words:

> I gave this writing the title "The Kingdom That Went to Ruin" because I had happened to read about an African kingdom that had gone to ruin in the evening edition of that day's newspaper. "The fading of a noble kingdom," the article went, "is much more melancholic than the fall of a second-rate republic."[7]

An individual who had been a faultless middle-class youth in his college days behaves in an "insincere" manner toward an actress who had been his friend for the sake of his company job. What is more, he keeps wearing a pleasant smile even when he is publicly humiliated by the enraged actress. Although members of the middle class in contemporary Japan are far more materially wealthy than China's Ah Q in the days of the Chinese Revolution, the narrator must have felt that they are, like Ah Q, paralyzed in spirit. In his youth, the son of a middle-class family appears to the narrator like the successor of a "noble kingdom." But after working as an elite employee and becoming the successor of his kingdom, the impression he gives the narrator is faded and melancholic.

Criticism of the national character and despair as common themes

Another twelve years later, in June 1994, Murakami traveled to the site of the 1939 Nomonhan Incident to do research for book three of *The Wind-Up Bird Chronicle*. In a travelogue that he wrote after returning home, he criticized the foundations of the "democratic state," or the middle-class society, that was formed in postwar Japan.

> After the war ended, the Japanese came to hate war and to love peace (or, more precisely, *being in peace*). We have been striving to break through the Japanese state's *inefficiency*, which ultimately led Japan to catastrophe, as something that is outdated. Instead of questioning the responsibility of the inefficiency within us, we treated it as something that has been imposed on us from the outside by sheer force and disposed of it simply and physically, as if by surgery. As a result, we have certainly come to live in an efficient world founded on the principles of modern civil society, and that efficiency has brought overwhelming prosperity to our society.
>
> Yet I (and perhaps many others) find it difficult to brush off the vague suspicion that even now, at many junctures in society, we are being

eliminated quietly and peacefully as nameless consumables.[8]

Lu Xun's "The True Story of Ah Q" and Murakami's "The Kingdom That Went to Ruin" share the theme of criticism of the national character. Furthermore, both authors hold particularly deep sentiments for the protagonist, each of whom expresses his convoluted feelings at the beginning of the story. Here's Lu Xun:

> For several years now I have been meaning to write the true story of Ah Q. But while wanting to write I was in some trepidation, too, which goes to show I am not one of those who achieve glory by writing. . . . But in the end, as though possessed by some fiend, I always come back to the idea of writing the story of Ah Q.[9]

And here's Murakami:

> Each time I try to tell somebody about Mr. Q, I'm struck by a hopeless sense of impotence. I've never been good at explaining things, but even taking that into account, explaining Mr. Q's character is a peculiar task, and an almost impossible one at that. And each time I give it a try, I'm seized with a deep, deep, deep, deep feeling of despair.[10]

The original Chinese text of "as though possessed by some fiend" can be literally translated: "as if there is a ghost in my mind." The despair of Murakami's protagonist, which he expresses by repeating "deep" four times, is analogous to the self-awareness of Lu Xun's narrator of being possessed by Ah Q's ghost.

The long version of Murakami's 1991 short story "Tony Takitani" ["Toni Takitani"] depicts a father who spent his youth as a jazzman in Japanese-occupied Shanghai and his son, whospent his youth as an illustrator in Tokyo during the postwar period of high economic growth. The father, Shozaburo, "took it easy all through the upheaval of the war—from the Japanese invasion of China to the attack on Pearl Harbor to the dropping of two atomic bombs—playing his trombone in Shanghai nightclubs. . . . Shozaburo Takitani was a man who possessed not the slightest hint of will or introspection with regard to history."[11] He might be framed as the pre–World War II Japanese version of Ah Q. As for his son, Tony, "While the young people around him were anguishing over which paths they should follow in life" in the days of the campus riots of the late 1960s, "he went on doing his precise mechanical drawings without a thought for anything else" [p. 180]. He is the Ah Q of postwar Japan, as well as an alter ego of Mr. Q in "The Kingdom That Went to Ruin." I will reserve a fuller discussion of "Tony Takitani" for a future article.

In this essay I have attempted to shed light on

the genealogical ties between the authors Lu Xun and Haruki Murakami, a connection previously shrouded in darkness. The impact of both authors has extended beyond East Asia to the world. By unraveling the genealogical ties between them, we may be able to form a theoretical framework for compiling a history of twentieth-century East Asian literature. The East Asian legacy of the Ah Q image invented by Lu Xun has been passed on via Haruki Murakami to the Hong Kong film director Wong Kar-wai—a topic that I hope to explore in a future writing.

Endnotes

[1] For a biography of Lu Xun and a history of studies on the author, see Shozo Fujii, *Ro Jin jiten* [The Lu Xun Encyclopedia] (Tokyo: Sanseido Publishing, 2002).

[2] Jay Rubin, *Haruki Murakami to kotoba no ongaku*, trans. Kazuyo Kuroyanagi (Tokyo: Shinchosha Publishing, 2006), 444; originally published as *Haruki Murakami and the Music of Words* (London: Harvill Press, 2002).

[3] See Shozo Fujii, "Chugoku no naka no Murakami Haruki" [The Haruki Murakami within China], parts 1–8, *Issatsu no hon* (Asahi Shimbun Sha), September 2006–April 2007, and "Murakami Haruki no naka no Chugoku" [The China within Haruki Murakami], parts 1–3, *UP* (University of Tokyo Press), May 2006–July 2006.

[4] Haruki Murakami, *Hear the Wind Sing*, trans. Alfred Birnbaum (Tokyo: Kodansha, 1987), 5.

[5] William Tay, "I was somewhat of a rebel: An interview of the Japanese novelist Haruki Murakami," in *Lian He Wen Xue*, January 1993: 40.

[6] Haruki Murakami, "Hon no hanashi (3): Tsuke de hon o kau koto ni tsuite" [Discussing books, no. 3: About Buying Books

on Credit], in *Murakami Asahi-do* (Tokyo: Shincho Bunko, 1987), 136.

[7] Haruki Murakami, *Murakami Haruki zen sakuhin 1979–1989 5* [The Complete Works of Haruki Murakami, 1979–1989, volume five] (Tokyo: Kodansha, 1991), 113–20.

[8] Haruki Murakami, *Henkyo, kinkyo* [Remote Lands, Close Distances] (Tokyo: Shinchosha Publishing, 2000), 140.

[9] Lu Xun, *The True Story of Ah Q*, trans. Yang Xianyi and Gladys Yang (Hong Kong: The Chinese University Press, 2002), 2.

[10] *Complete Works 5*, 115–116.

[11] Haruki Murakami, "Tony Takitani," in *Blind Willow, Sleeping Woman*, trans. Jay Rubin (London: Harvill Secker, 2006), 175–76.

The Other Side of Happiness: Acting in *Tony Takitani*

Issey Ogata

For thirty years I have been performing monodramas in which I portray a variety of characters on the stage by acting out people's exteriors. I had always thought it a natural choice to create personas through differences in facial features and physique, but it seems that approaching roles from the outside is very unconventional. In my occasional stints on screen I find that my serious efforts are denied: "Please act naturally," people say; "Could you do it with a normal look?"

When I taught acting at a German drama school, the young actors grew excited as I told them to stick out their chins, walk with their toes turned in, or throw back their heads. Being excited is fine; but it was as if they thought they were doing a comic skit. This resulted only in stereotypical forms like "a cranky old person," "an introvert," or "a bossy man." It was no use suggesting that there are extroverts who walk with their toes turned in.

To get students to develop roles more subtly, I had them look into a mirror and twist their cheeks and mouths. I wanted them to discover in the mirror someone other than themselves. But the students roared their disapproval, saying that if you create an emotion, it will naturally show in your facial expression and gestures. They believed that first there is the mind, which is then manifested in the body, while we feel that the inside is projected by our assuming the superficial features. In simple terms, you might think of it as a divide along the lines of the much-debated question of whether you cry because you feel sad or you feel sad because you cry.

A role that defies monodramatic techniques

When I was chosen to play the part of Tony Takitani in a film, my first impression of the story "Tony Takitani" was that it has an odd title. Tony sounds like an

American nickname, whereas Takitani is a dignified, noble-sounding Japanese surname. As one who sculpts personas from superficialities, I was struck by how, in spite of the saying "Name and nature often agree," the man's name seemed to give no hint of his character. The author, Haruki Murakami, has written that he was inspired by a logo T-shirt printed with the name, which he saw at a tourist beach. But bound by the knowledge that Tony Takitani was a real-life individual, all I could imagine was the logo under the blazing sun and nothing of his nature.

In "Tony Takitani," Tony's father, who gave him his name, flees an increasingly militaristic Japan on the eve of World War II and poses as a stateless jazzman in Shanghai, where he is imprisoned on charges of espionage. Analytically speaking, the man is taken captive by his Japanese citizenship in spite of having chosen to forsake his nationality, an externally prescribed label. I was to play the role of Tony's jazzman father as well.

The focal point of the story is Tony's wife's clothes—a straightforward superficiality. No sooner does Tony try to put the brakes on his wife's excessive penchant for buying clothes than she dies. This seems to suggest that she has been defining herself entirely in terms of the clothes covering her externally. Tony foolishly tries to have an assistant wear the piles of clothes that his wife has left behind. I was moved by that part of the story, all the more so because the script says that

this is just a whim. After reading the story, I felt there was nothing strange in assuming that a person is replaceable if the superficialities are taken to be the entirety of an individual.

Director Jun Ichikawa's request prior to filming the story was to "not act." This was clearly distinct from earlier demands by other directors, who wanted me to "act naturally." Listening to Ichikawa, I got the idea that he was asking me not to force the protagonist into a category. After all, this was a man with the name Tony Takitani. My monodramatic technique of determining a character's appearance and personality by the distortions of his occupation would not be of much use. Rather, the challenge would be one of depicting a personality pattern that has no social model.

Taking care not to spill the brimming glass of water

The film was set on a hilltop, overlooking green hills beyond closely huddled houses. Although there were several panels serving as walls, there were no glass-paned windows; it was as if the outdoor space had literally merged with the room. The intent, it seems, was to depict an image contrary to that of an enclosed room. I could imagine that the protagonist was a man who did not mind having no privacy, but I wondered how the character was to be portrayed. For good or for ill, the weather remained fair during much of the loca-

tion shoot, in which natural phenomena were recorded on film exactly as they occurred.

In most of the scenes, the protagonist spends his time in this featureless room. Here he works, he eats, he receives phone calls. I had to attempt expressions conveying that he feels it is only natural not to connect with others. They are expressions of affluence at the opposite extreme from solitude or loneliness, but I had to not act too much.

Once the shooting started, I did not find it particularly difficult to physicalize moves and words of the sort that are seemingly absorbed into the woodwork. All I had to do was concentrate on unintentional moves and words. For instance, there was a scene in which Tony took a block of tofu out of the refrigerator. If I had carried the tofu to the table, it would have become an act of preparing to eat. The acting needed to portray purely "taking out tofu" and nothing more. Ultimately, that scene became one of taking the tofu from the refrigerator, gazing at it for a while, and putting it back. This translates into "thinking of eating tofu but then quitting," but one might also imagine that Tony just wanted to look at the tofu.*

The key to acting the part, I may say, was to take care not to spill the water that fills a brimming glass inside my body. But I could not be too careful, either. The

---

*For production reasons, the actual scene in the film is slightly different from what is described here.

glass of water is not visible from the outside; it must not be seen. So when I felt that something went well, it did not work for the film. The self-conscious act of exploring myself would have made the water spill over.

The director's courage in making a "heartless" film

One of the final scenes in the film is set in a room filled with the dead wife's clothes. It is a place Tony presumably has not set foot in before. The shell called clothing paradoxically makes one conscious of its substance, somewhat like imagining a person's face without the makeup. There are too many shells for Tony to relate to the contents of each, and the seemingly insensitive act of making another woman wear his wife's clothes or of selling them off may be his only way of facing up to them.

Perhaps Tony, who is unable to cry over his wife's death and is evidently unmoved by encounters with others, has always been burdened with heaps of empty shells. The room full of his wife's clothes turns into an empty space, and Tony experiences something akin to a sense of loss.

I respect the director for venturing to create *Tony Takitani* knowing that a movie with so little emotional expression would become a film devoid of humanity. I can only tip my hat to him, a director who is generally known for TV commercials, for having made a "heart-

less" film while taking the risk that people would think of it as simply an exercise in cinematic art. It may be that he had ambivalent thoughts as a creator of TV commercials, the vanguard of the mass-consumer society. I cannot help feeling that his position made him try to break through the externally prescribed label called clothes—if you will, to the other side of the happiness of owning products, the keystone of capitalism.

Though lasting emotions may not have been for this film, as an actor I regret that I wasn't able to fully convey the "fleeting moments of joy and sorrow." For I believe that while there was no guarantee of lasting happiness between Tony and his wife, there were many moments in which they understood each other in a flash.

Haruki Murakami as a Contemporary Phenomenon

Koichi Oi

During the more than a quarter of a century since winning the Gunzo Prize for New Writers in 1979 with *Hear the Wind Sing*, Haruki Murakami has seen his works translated into over thirty languages and has remained one of the most prominent figures in Japan's literary world. Such stature would normally prompt the media to view him as an establishment figure, but by no means has Murakami been portrayed and perceived as a conventional, "run of the mill" bestselling author.

He has been the target of both lavish praise and deep suspicion from literary critics, and the unique position he enjoys today is probably the product of a complex synthesis of arguments from both sides. My intention here is not to explore the literary merits of Murakami's works but to view his rise to stardom as a social phenomenon. I wish particularly to investigate the significance of this rise to the average Japanese, someone who has no special interest in literature. I will do so by tracing the way he has been portrayed in the media—not literary magazines and other specialist media but newspapers and magazines aimed at a general readership. This should give a clue as to how society has viewed him as a contemporary phenomenon.

To facilitate this task, I have classified Murakami's career, as depicted by the media, into five distinct periods.* The first is between 1979, when he made his literary debut, and 1984; the second is between 1985, when he won the Tanizaki Prize, and 1987, when he published his bestselling *Norwegian Wood*; the third is between 1988 and 1996, when he was awarded the Yomiuri Literary Prize; the fourth is between 1997, when he published *Underground*, and 2000, when he issued his short-story collection *after the quake*; and the fifth is 2001 to the present.

---

*Needless to say, these five periods reflect the media's portrayal of Murakami and do not represent distinct periods in his literary activity.

A *quiet debut*

Murakami's first appearance in the general press was in 1979, as noted above, when he won the twenty-second Gunzo Prize for New Writers. The winner was selected by a screening committee on April 9, and the decision was reported in the *Sankei Shimbun* newspaper the following day. It was a small, one-column story, and most other dailies also carried this piece of news over the next few days, giving it similarly minor treatment.[*] As far as the general media were concerned, Murakami did not receive special mention but was accorded the kind of treatment one would normally expect of any promising new author. There was one weekly magazine, though, that zeroed in on Murakami's occupation, which the dailies simply reported as "self-employed." In an interview published in its May 4 issue, *Shukan Asahi* ran a two-page spread titled "The Winner of the Gunzo Prize for New Writers, 29-Year-Old Haruki Murakami, Is a Jazz Cafe Owner with a Collection of 3,000 Albums." The article carried a photo

---

[*]Papers misspelled the name of the winner, using the wrong ideogram for the "ki" in Haruki. There is a possibility that this was intentional and that Murakami was using a pen name briefly at the start of his career. Incidentally, the Gunzo Prize for New Writers is also awarded to works of criticism, but no winner was selected in 1979. Two works were given honorable mentions, however—by Koichiro Tomioka and Kuniichi Uno, both of whom have since established themselves as distinguished writers.

of Murakami standing in front of a shelf packed with records and proclaimed, "The writer is the latest in a recent line of mold-breaking literary newcomers."

Two years later, in 1981, Murakami sold his café and devoted himself full-time to a writing career. While at this point he had published only two novels, *Hear the Wind Sing* and *Pinball, 1973*, his distinctive story-telling style had already gained the attention of such noted critics as Saburo Kawamoto, Takaaki Yoshimoto, and Toshiyuki Tsukimura, and he had developed a considerable following among younger readers. The general press, though, had yet to take serious notice of this phenomenon, about the only exception being a small, timely interview that appeared in the May 17, 1980, evening edition of the *Asahi Shimbun* newspaper under the headline "A Writer Enjoys a Quiet Boom among the Younger Generation." He also contributed a feature to the *Asahi*'s November 12, 1980, evening edition, "The Appeal of F. Scott Fitzgerald."

A breath of fresh air

Murakami's next wave of appearances in the press came in 1982, after he won the fourth Noma Literary Prize for New Writers for *A Wild Sheep Chase* (originally published in the August 1982 issue of the magazine *Gunzo* and as an independent volume in October that year). Newspaper coverage of the award ceremony

in December, though, focused more on Nobuo Kojima, who won the prize in the category for established writers, a fact that appears rather surprising in hindsight.

Press coverage of Murakami around this time began focusing on his "eccentric lifestyle." A February 20, 1983, article in the *Sankei Shimbun*, for instance, discussed his odd habit of digging a hole in the backyard of his house in Funabashi, Chiba Prefecture, only to fill it in again. And the May 1 edition of the *Mainichi Shimbun* newspaper described him as living a "craftsmanlike life," not owning a television set or a car and never traveling abroad. While the two articles gave rather contrasting images of the author, both portrayed him as a "new hope" whose works had brought a breath of fresh air into the literary world.

The most important media article in this period is no doubt the one published in the May 25, 1984, issue of the weekly *Asahi Journal*. Murakami was the seventh to appear in a popular series of interviews conducted by chief editor (and now newscaster) Tetsuya Chikushi with figures "revered" by young people. Because of the high visibility of this series, the article helped make Murakami a household name among a broad segment of young people who were not particularly avid fans of literature.

The magazine devoted five pages to the article, in which Murakami gave detailed responses to Chikushi's probing questions, including those about his experiences with the student protest movement. One of the

more interesting comments he made during the interview was, "I feel that someday I'll need to come to terms with my involvement in that movement during the 1970s." The article was accompanied by many photographs illustrating Murakami's lifestyle and personality, including shots of him holding his cat and jogging (the caption to the latter read, "I run 10 kilometers a day"), as well as a photo of his study crammed with LPs and cassette tapes.

A Murakami boom

So far I have discussed the first period of Murakami's career. The reason I chose to begin the second period with his 1985 *Hard-Boiled Wonderland and the End of the World* (which won the twenty-first Tanizaki Prize) is that this is when he began to appear in the general media with far greater frequency. Because space is limited, I will touch upon this period only briefly, but I would note that considerable media attention was focused on his youth. A September 26, 1985, article in the *Tokyo Shimbun* newspaper, for example, reported that Murakami was the first winner of the Tanizaki Prize to be born after World War II. Many people viewed the awarding of this prize—usually given to critically acclaimed works by well-known writers—to "the first 'pure literature' novelist in a long time to sell well and to have a strong following among younger readers"

(*Sankei Shimbun*, evening edition, September 25) as the literary establishment's recognition of his talent. The public may have been less interested in his "urban, sophisticated writing style" (*Asahi Shimbun*, morning edition, October 20) than in his quirkiness, such as his penchant for moving home on a whim and his refusal to appear at lectures, on TV and radio, and in commercials (*Tokyo Shimbun*, evening edition, October 5).

His widening appeal to not just his core of rapturous fans but to a segment of the public with varying degrees of interest in him laid the groundwork for the appearance of the "Murakami phenomenon" (*Mainichi Shimbun*, morning edition, November 18). A full-fledged "Murakami boom" (*Mainichi Shimbun*, morning edition, December 19) arrived in the third period following the publication of *Norwegian Wood*. Thereafter, Murakami's works regularly made the bestseller list, and his overwhelming popularity came to be viewed as news in itself, engendering such media buzzwords as "the Haruki-Banana phenomenon" (in reference to Banana Yoshimoto) and "the double Murakami phenomenon" (in reference to Ryu Murakami). Ironically, Murakami spent most of this period in the United States and Europe, dedicating his time to writing, quite removed from the commotion his works were causing in Japan.

He decided to return in 1995, though, following the January 17 Kobe earthquake and the March 20 sarin gas poisoning in the Tokyo subways, marking a

conscious swing, as he noted, from social "detachment to commitment." This is his fourth period, which was centered on works of nonfiction, such as his startling *Underground.*

Now, at the turn of the twenty-first century, Murakami occupies a place that no Japanese writer has ever before attained—recognition as a writer of global stature. This can be easily gleaned from the intense media reaction in Europe, North America, and across Asia that greeted the 2002 publication of *Kafka on the Shore.*

Contemporary Japanese Literature Finds a Global Following

Shinya Machida

Japanese novels are increasingly attracting an international readership. This is my impression as a newspaper reporter covering literary news, based on the growing number of articles describing the favorable reaction to these novels in foreign countries. Let me cite a few examples.

In 2004 the mystery writer Natsuo Kirino's novel *Out* became the first Japanese work to be nominated for the Edgar Allan Poe Award for best novel, presented

each year by the Mystery Writers of America. The novel tells how a battered housewife kills her husband and dismembers his body with the help of colleagues at her late-night, part-time job and the process by which they together become social outcasts. *Publishers Weekly* proclaimed that "the gritty realism of everyday existence in the underbelly of Japan's consumer society comes across with pungent force." In short, a mystery written for the Japanese domestic market was recognized as being capable of generating an international following.

Also in 2004, three horror novels by Koji Suzuki were published in the United States: *Ring*, *Spiral*, and *Dark Water*. This came on the heels of the box-office success in 2002 of the Hollywood remake of the movie *Ring*, which grossed $128 million. In 2005 Penguin Books paid tens of thousands of dollars for the English-language publishing rights to Hitomi Kanehara's Akutagawa Prize–winning *Snakes and Earrings*.

An even bigger global literary presence, needless to say, is Haruki Murakami, whose works have been translated into over thirty languages. When the English translation of *Kafka on the Shore* was published in 2005, it became an immediate bestseller. When a senior colleague of mine visited London in May 2006, he observed that this and Murakami's *The Wind-Up Bird Chronicle* were displayed prominently near the entrance of a London bookstore. Murakami, he realized, was being read just like English-speaking writers.

Exporting entertainment

Japan has a huge deficit in literary trade, especially with Western countries. A survey conducted in 1999 by the Japan Foundation found that twenty times more foreign titles were being translated into Japanese than vice versa. What accounts for the recent shift in this trend?

The first factor is the increase in the number of Japanese novels with high entertainment value. Most literary works hitherto translated into foreign languages were in the genre of "pure literature," such as novels by Kenzaburo Oe, Yukio Mishima, and Yasunari Kawabata. By contrast, recent interest has been focused on mysteries, horror stories, and works portraying the urban lifestyle of young people.

Since 1988 Takarajimasha, Inc. has been publishing a book at the end of each year introducing the best mystery novels for that year. This publication has been drawing increasing attention in recent years, suggesting that there has been considerable maturing of works in the mystery, horror, fantasy, and other entertainment genres. This may have paved the way for the growing readership of Japanese novels in foreign markets.

Another factor is the rising interest in Japanese culture due to the popularity of *manga* and *anime*, among the most successful examples being *Spirited Away*, a film by Hayao Miyazaki that captured the Golden Bear at the Berlin International Film Festival in 2002 and

the Academy Award for Best Animated Feature Film in 2003, and *Dragon Ball*, a *manga* series by Akira Toriyama that has sold some 13 million copies internationally.

The major publisher Shueisha initiated full-fledged *manga* publication activities outside Japan in 1993, engendering a boom first in South Korea, Taiwan, and other Asian markets, and then in France, Italy, and ultimately the United States, where it launched an English-language version of the monthly *manga* magazine *Shonen Jump* in 2002, feeding the rapidly rising *manga* craze there. Exports of Japan's popular literature have been fueled by the growing number of young people fascinated by "cool Japan."

Consumers are not the only ones who are being drawn to Japanese literature; it is also attracting the interest of filmmakers in Hollywood and elsewhere, who have been confronted with a shortage of original works that can be adapted to the screen. Several remakes of Japanese films were released in 2004 and 2005, including Takashi Shimizu's horror flick *The Grudge* (with Hollywood financing the director's own adaptation), *Shall We Dance?* starring Richard Gere, and *Dark Water*, based on a short story by Koji Suzuki. These films suggest that US movie producers have run short of domestic works suited to screen adaptation and have begun to look to new sources, including Japanese literary works, to generate box-office hits.

New opportunities

How are Japanese publishers responding to this golden opportunity? Many major publishing houses, unfortunately, seem to believe that only *manga* will sell overseas and have not been marketing novels very aggressively. One reason for the focus on *manga* is that because of serialization a single hit is capable of generating huge profits through multivolume sales and proceeds from character-related merchandise. A novel, these publishers contend, does not have the same profit-generating potential.

There are enterprising individuals, though, who have filled an international marketing niche that large publishers have largely neglected, one of them being Hiroki Sakai, who founded Vertical, Inc. in the United States to translate and publish Japanese novels in English. After working as an editor in the publishing division of the *Nihon Keizai Shimbun* newspaper, he traveled to the United States in 1998 to learn why Japanese novels were not being more eagerly read abroad. To date, Vertical has published a series of works by Koji Suzuki, the romance *Twinkle Twinkle* by Kaori Ekuni, and many other contemporary novels. *Twinkle Twinkle* has been retranslated into seven European languages and has been generating steady sales.

Sakai has a very clear policy on choosing which works to translate: they must belong to an identifiable genre; have a logical construction; not require any

special knowledge of Japan; and be capable of screen adaptation. These criteria show that Sakai is clearly looking for works that have entertainment value for foreign readers and can be made into movies or television dramas.

In the case of Japanese films, royalties for the original work run from several hundred thousand yen to about three million yen. In the United States, however, it is normal to allocate 2 percent of total production costs to the original work. In the case of a Hollywood megaproduction costing $100 million or more, therefore, it is not inconceivable for the author to receive $2 million for a single book.

Finding good translators

There are many hurdles, though, that must be cleared before Japanese literature can be successfully marketed in foreign countries. The market for translated works of fiction in the United States is only around 2–3 percent of its total book market. The Japanese literary boom in France and other European countries, moreover, must be viewed in the context of a general heightening of interest in the literature of other countries. And there are still few people in Japan who fully understand and can map out a marketing strategy for the US book market, about half of which is now dominated by Random House, Penguin, and other oligopolistic publishers.

An even bigger issue is the shortage of capable translators. In the postwar years Japan benefited from the presence of scholars like Donald Keene, who had close personal contact with leading Japanese novelists, including Yukio Mishima and Kobo Abe, and Edward Seidensticker, who translated the classic *Tale of Genji*.

The literature of a foreign country cannot be truly appreciated without good translations. A number of public-sector projects have been launched to encourage the spread of Japanese literature abroad. Among the best known are the Translation and Publication Support Program of the Japan Foundation and the Japanese Literature Publishing Project, launched in 2002 by the Agency for Cultural Affairs. The latter program has thus far financed the translation of sixty-one works, ranging from Soseki Natsume's *Botchan* to Amy Yamada's *Bedtime Eyes*, into English, French, Russian, and/or German. This may be a rather small scale project at present, but it is nonetheless a very valuable initiative and ought to be expanded.

Stimulating creative activity

I believe that Japanese literature needs to make further inroads into foreign markets, even if this means surmounting formidable obstacles. One reason is that it would stimulate creative activity among Japanese writers. The US book market, at 2.6 trillion yen, is twice the

size of the domestic market, while the European market is around two trillion yen. Generating sales in such mammoth markets would be a boon for both publishers and writers. Because of the recent decline in book readership in Japan, many publishing firms have been decreasing the size of initial print runs. This means that good books are reaching fewer readers and authors' royalties are falling. Appealing to a global market could reverse this trend.

A second reason is that fuller exposure to Japanese fiction could stimulate literary activity among foreign writers. Works by the nineteenth-century Russian writer Fyodor Dostoevsky, for example, have continued to have a profound effect on Japanese writers from Yutaka Haniya, a prominent postwar literary figure, to Fuminori Nakamura, winner of the 2005 Akutagawa Prize. World literature has evolved as works written in different countries cross-fertilize one another. Much remains to be done by writers, publishers, the government, and others before Japanese literature can claim a part in this global movement.

The Making of "A Wild Haruki Chase"

Murakami Books Worldwide

About the Contributors

The Making
of "A Wild Haruki Chase"

A SYMPOSIUM WITH TRANSLATORS FROM AROUND
THE WORLD

Koji Sato, Japan Foundation

The seeds for the symposium "A Wild Haruki Chase:
How the World Is Reading and Translating Murakami"
were sown more than two years ago. One day, several
Japan Foundation staff members were discussing cultural exchange with Inuhiko Yomota, a professor at
Meiji Gakuen University, when he gave us the idea that
became the basis for the symposium.

We knew intuitively that this would be an exciting event. But since there were few precedents for
international symposiums dealing with a still-active
author, we took time to think through the aims and
the method of giving the idea form. In the course of
that process, we put together a project team with four
wonderful navigators. In addition to Yomota, whose
interests range from film studies to literary criticism,
they included Mitsuyoshi Numano, a scholar of Russian literature who follows the reception of Haruki
Murakami in Russia and Eastern Europe; Motoyuki
Shibata, a scholar of Anglo-American literature who
is also known as Murakami's partner in English-to-
Japanese translation; and Shozo Fujii, who special-

125

izes in Chinese literature and is conducting the joint research project "East Asia and Haruki Murakami." This was in February 2005.

Guided by these advisors, we decided on two objectives: to make the symposium a translation festival featuring translators in order to identify the diverse ways in which Murakami's works are being read via the process of translation and to explore what aspects of Murakami's literary world are winning the sympathy of those on the receiving end. We decided to make this an opportunity to contemplate the possibilities for the acceptance of contemporary literature across national borders in the global age—as well as the difficulty of having the locality of Japanese literature and culture, with the exception of Murakami's works, accepted across borders.

At the main symposium in Tokyo, translators from different countries presented their distinctive views of Murakami. It was a moving experience. Expressing her thoughts as a Murakami fan, the Taiwanese translator Lai Ming-Chu observed that the "margins" in Murakami's works are a playground for both author and reader where the reader can enjoy various interpretations inside a virtual tunnel. I understood this to be a comment representing the Taiwanese readers who have been moved by her heartfelt translations. Jay Rubin of the United States, who had been studying modern Japanese literature by such writers as Ryunosuke Akutagawa and had read very little contemporary

literature, was blown away by the rich imaginative power of Murakami's literary world the first time he read something by Murakami and became a passionate translator of his works. Behind the mask of a university professor was the face of a youthful literature buff, and I sensed the great power of fine literature in appealing to diverse people across differences of age and occupation.

Dmitry Kovalenin of Russia observed that "the Murakami world is a mix of text, music (rhythm), and film, and at the core of that complex lies the heart." This brought home to me the way in which the media-mix modernity of Murakami's literary universe has attracted a wide range of readers. I also felt strongly that the real reason behind the Murakami boom is his fundamental engagement with matters of the heart as a central literary theme. With regard to this issue of ties of the heart, I would like to thank Richard Powers for shedding light on the universal appeal of Murakami's works using the cutting-edge science of mirror neurons.

Kim Choon Mie of South Korea noted, "Haruki is an exception in Japanese literature, which has continued to be treated as 'foreign literature' in South Korea because of the history between the two countries, and he has won the sympathy of many South Koreans as an author who earnestly looks at Japan's past deeds in Asia." The revelation of how greatly a single author is contributing to the grave issue of historical reconciliation no doubt came as a surprise to the audience.

In many non-Western countries there is also the question of what "I" should live by after a major chapter in the country's history has come to an end, its youth having fought for political democratization and experienced disillusion. The analysis was made that Murakami's works touch the hearts of youth in newly democratized Asian countries and in post-Soviet Russia because the state of Japanese society underlying his works resonates with the upheavals that have occurred in the societies where his works are read. To ordinary people who are disconcerted by the rapid urbanization and the system of mass consumption around them, his works seemingly serve as bibles that speak to the isolation of urban life.

In return for their wonderful gift to Japanese lovers of literature and Murakami fans, the Japan Foundation presented the translators with an overnight stay by Lake Yamanaka, where they experienced the luxuriant nature around Mount Fuji, lectures on contemporary Japanese literature by Chikara Suzuki of the publisher Shinchosha and Koichi Oi of Mainichi Newspapers, and a network of friends with whom they can communicate in the future.

During their stay, the translators engaged in conversations about Murakami day and night. They excitedly shared their opinions when the discussion turned to the subject of which novel they liked best. It was a tough trial for me, a neophyte fan of Murakami who began to read his works only after becoming involved

in the project. But as I watched the translators rekindling their excitement by accurately citing their favorite scenes and lines, I renewed my conviction that Murakami no longer belongs to the Japanese alone.

On the day of our departure from Lake Yamanaka, we paid a visit to the nearby Mishima Yukio Museum. We were overjoyed by one of the photographs on display: it depicted a public debate between Mishima and Zenkyoto (All-Campus Joint Struggle Committee) at the University of Tokyo, and the venue was Classroom 900, where the symposium "A Wild Haruki Chase" had been held. We posed for a commemorative photo in front of the museum with the presentiment that the symposium, for which translators had gathered from around the world during the cherry blossom season of 2006, will one day become another page in history.

A VISIT TO MURAKAMI'S ALMA MATER

Ayumi Hashimoto, Japan Foundation

The Kobe symposium was held at Kobe High School, Haruki Murakami's alma mater. Over 150 people participated even though it was a weekday. The keynote speaker and host of the symposium was Inuhiko Yomota, and the panelists were Kim Choon Mie of South Korea, Leung Ping-kwan of Hong Kong, Tomas Jurkovic of the Czech Republic, and Ted Goossen of Canada.

Prior to the symposium, the panelists walked around the neighborhood where Murakami had lived. It was an informative and rewarding experience as translators and scholars, they said, to have been able to actually visit Murakami's middle school and the library that he used to frequent. It was noted during the symposium that the fact that Murakami was born in Kobe greatly influences his works, as does the city's nature as a port open to other countries.

The Kobe program was graced with the participation of Murakami's classmates from Kobe High School, invaluable witnesses to what he was like in his high school days. According to them, the young Murakami was a fashionable person, his hair grown out—unusual for men and boys at the time—and wearing a button-down shirt and well-polished shoes. He was also very good at English, they said. When they first heard about Murakami's novels they thought the author was someone else with the same name, and they could not help exclaiming in surprise when they found out that it was the same Murakami that they had known. The humorous and witty talk by Murakami's classmates sparked much laughter.

The audience listened intently to the proceedings. In the questionnaire that they filled out after the symposium, Murakami fans wrote that they felt motivated to reread his works with a fresh perspective, while participants who were unacquainted with his works wrote that they wanted to give them a try. Although the

symposium has ended, each individual's "wild Haruki chase" looks set to continue for a while yet.

SATISFACTION FOR ALL AT THE "SECRET MAIN EVENT"

Aya Tamura, Japan Foundation

Four of the international participants in the symposium "A Wild Haruki Chase" flew to Sapporo, the destination of "I" and "she" in *A Wild Sheep Chase*. They were to take part in a symposium held under the joint sponsorship of the Japan Foundation and Hokkaido University's Slavic Research Center following the Tokyo program and a stay by Lake Yamanaka. The members were Jay Rubin of the United States, Dmitry Kovalenin of Russia, Lai Ming-Chu of Taiwan, and Anna Zielinska-Elliott of Poland. Kovalenin appeared in a wool vest in tribute to the key motif of sheep that links Murakami's novel with the land of Hokkaido.

The main event of the stay in Hokkaido was of course the symposium, but there was another incident that the participants called the "secret main event": an excursion to a hotel that is rumored to have been the model for the Dolphin Hotel that appears in *A Wild Sheep Chase*. The initial plan was simply to view the hotel from inside the bus on the morning of the symposium. But at the strong request of the translators, it was decided to actually visit the hotel.

Upon entering the lobby, we all began looking around curiously. Soon someone discovered on the floor map that there is actually a bar on the top floor, just as in the novel—except that this hotel has twenty-five stories, whereas the Dolphin Hotel in the novel has twenty-four. So we took the elevator and visited the bar. The bar was closed, since it was early in the day, but we asked the staff to let us in, and we finished off with a commemorative photo at the counter. The translators look very contented in the photograph. Everyone was convinced that this was none other than the Dolphin Hotel, and they were more delighted here than anywhere else in Sapporo. One of the translators asked why we did not let them stay at this hotel.

At the symposium, which was held in the afternoon, the translators' discussion delved into the differences between the Sapporo that they had imagined from reading Murakami's novel and their impressions of the actual city, as well as the significance of Hokkaido in Murakami's work. Around two hundred people attended despite the snow, and the enthusiastic audience asked many questions about the niceties of translation. The Sapporo symposium was a lively and fruitful event featuring discussions that could have taken place only in this northern city.

OUTLINE OF SYMPOSIUMS AND WORKSHOPS

A Wild Haruki Chase: How the World Is Reading and Translating Murakami

Facilitators

Motoyuki Shibata (Professor, University of Tokyo)

Mitsuyoshi Numano (Professor, University of Tokyo)

Shozo Fujii (Professor, University of Tokyo)

Inuhiko Yomota (Professor, Meiji Gakuin University)

Keynote speaker: Richard Powers (American novelist)

Translators and critics (in alphabetical order):

Corinne Atlan (France)

Alfred Birnbaum (United States)

Angel Bojadsen (Brazil)

Ted Goossen (Canada)

Erdos György (Hungary)

Uwe Hohmann (Germany)

Mette Holm (Denmark)

Jonjon Johana (Indonesia)

Tomas Jurkovic (Czech Republic)

Ika Kaminka (Norway)

Kim Choon Mie (Korea)

Dmitry Kovalenin (Russia)

Lai Ming-Chu (Taiwan)

Pham Huu Loi (Vietnam)

Leung Ping-kwan (Hong Kong)

Ivan Logatchov (Russia)
Serguei Logatchev (Russia)
Jay Rubin (United States)
Ye Hui (Malaysia)

Tokyo Program, March 25–26, 2006

VENUE Komaba Campus, University of Tokyo
ORGANIZED BY The Japan Foundation
CO-ORGANIZED BY Mainichi Newspapers
With the cooperation of University of Tokyo

Public Symposium

KEYNOTE SPEAKER Richard Powers
PANEL DISCUSSION BY Translators from Around the
    World
LECTURE "Book-Jacket Designs Around the World: A
    Comparison of Japan's Image"
LECTURE "Haruki in Moving Images"

Workshops

WORKSHOP "The Joy of Murakami's Works: From the
    Perspective of Translation"
WORKSHOP "The Murakami Boom and Globalization:
    Is This Japonisme or Universal Literature?"

Kobe Program, March 29, 2006

ORGANIZED BY The Japan Foundation, Kobe Municipal Government, and Kobe High School
COMMEMORATIVE SYMPOSIUM ON THE PREPARATIONS FOR THE KOBE CITY MUSEUM OF LITERATURE "A Wild Haruki Chase: How the World Is Reading and Translating Murakami"

Sapporo Program, March 29, 2006

ORGANIZED BY The Japan Foundation and the Slavic Research Center of Hokkaido University
SYMPOSIUM "A Wild Haruki Chase: How the World Is Reading and Translating Murakami"

Murakami Books Worldwide

Following the 1989 publication of *A Wild Sheep Chase* in English and of *Norwegian Wood* in Korean, Haruki Murakami came to be widely translated in the 1990s. The number of published translations has risen exponentially in the current decade, and books by Murakami are now available in more than forty languages. Here we survey the publication of ten major works in thirty-seven countries and regions across the world.

The symbol ✦ indicates works that were translated and/or published with support from the Japan Foundation.

Japan

A Wild Sheep Chase [Hitsuji o meguru boken], 1982

Hard-Boiled Wonderland and the End of the World [Sekai no owari to hadoboirudo wandarando], 1985

Norwegian Wood [Noruwei no mori], 1987

Dance Dance Dance [Dansu dansu dansu], 1988

South of the Border, West of the Sun [Kokkyo no minami, taiyo no nishi], 1992

The Wind-Up Bird Chronicle [Nejimaki-dori kuronikuru], 1992–95

Underground [Andaguraundo], 1997

The Place that was Promised [Yakusoku sareta basho de], 1998*
Sputnik Sweetheart [Suputoniku no koibito], 1999
Kafka on the Shore [Umibe no Kafuka], 2002
After Dark [Afuta Daku], 2004

Brazil

A Wild Sheep Chase, 2001
Dance Dance Dance, 2005
Norwegian Wood, 2005

Britain

A Wild Sheep Chase, 1990
Hard-Boiled Wonderland and the End of the World, 1991
Dance Dance Dance, 1994
The Wind-Up Bird Chronicle, 1998
South of the Border, West of the Sun, 1999
Norwegian Wood, 2000
Underground: The Tokyo Gas Attack and the Japanese Psyche, 2000
Sputnik Sweetheart, 2001
Kafka on the Shore, 2005

Underground and *The Place That Was Promised* were later combined to form the English-language book, *Underground: The Tokyo Gas Attack and the Japanese Psyche.*

Bulgaria

Norwegian Wood, 2005
Sputnik Sweetheart, 2005

China

Hard-Boiled Wonderland and the End of the World, 1996
Norwegian Wood, 1996
Dance Dance Dance, 1996
A Wild Sheep Chase, 1997
The Wind-Up Bird Chronicle, 1997
South of the Border, West of the Sun, 2001
Sputnik Sweetheart, 2001
Kafka on the Shore, 2003
After Dark, 2005

Croatia

Sputnik Sweetheart, 2002
South of the Border, West of the Sun, 2003

Czech Republic

Norwegian Wood, 2002
South of the Border, West of the Sun, 2004

Denmark

A Wild Sheep Chase, 1996
Dance Dance Dance, 1996
The Wind-up Bird Chronicle, 2000
South of the Border, West of the Sun, 2003
Sputnik Sweetheart, 2004
Norwegian Wood, 2005 ✦

Estonia

South of the Border, West of the Sun, 2003

Finland

A Wild Sheep Chase, 1992
Sputnik Sweetheart, 2003

France

A Wild Sheep Chase, 1990
Hard-Boiled Wonderland and the End of the World, 1992
Norwegian Wood, 1994
Dance Dance Dance, 1995
The Wind-Up Bird Chronicle, 2001
South of the Border, West of the Sun, 2002
Sputnik Sweetheart, 2003
Kafka on the Shore, 2005
After Dark, 2007

Germany

A Wild Sheep Chase, 1991
Hard-Boiled Wonderland and the End of the World, 1996
The Wind-Up Bird Chronicle, 1999
South of the Border, West of the Sun, 2000
Norwegian Wood, 2001
Dance Dance Dance, 2002
Underground, 2002
Sputnik Sweetheart, 2002
Kafka on the Shore, 2004
After Dark, 2005

Greece

A Wild Sheep Chase, 1991
Hard-Boiled Wonderland and the End of the World, 1994
The Wind-Up Bird Chronicle, 2005

Hong Kong

Norwegian Wood, 1991
A Wild Sheep Chase, 1992
Dance Dance Dance, 1992
South of the Border, West of the Sun, 1993
Hard-Boiled Wonderland and the End of the World, 1994

The Wind-Up Bird Chronicle, 1995
Sputnik Sweetheart, 1999
Kafka on the Shore, 2003
After Dark, 2005

Hungary

Hard-Boiled Wonderland and the End of the World,
   1998

Iceland

South of the Border, West of the Sun, 2001
Sputnik Sweetheart, 2003

Indonesia

Norwegian Wood, 2005

Israel

Norwegian Wood, 2000
South of the Border, West of the Sun, 2001
Underground, 2002
Sputnik Sweetheart, 2003
A Wild Sheep Chase, 2004
The Wind-Up Bird Chronicle, 2005

Italy

A Wild Sheep Chase, 1992
Norwegian Wood, 1993
Dance Dance Dance, 1998
The Wind-Up Bird Chronicle, 1999
South of the Border, West of the Sun, 2000
Sputnik Sweetheart, 2001
Hard-Boiled Wonderland and the End of the World,
    2002
Underground, 2003

Korea

Norwegian Wood, 1989
Dance Dance Dance, 1989
South of the Border, West of the Sun, 1993
The Wind-Up Bird Chronicle, 1994
Hard-Boiled Wonderland and the End of the World,
    1996
A Wild Sheep Chase, 1997
Underground, 1998
Sputnik Sweetheart, 1999
Kafka on the Shore, 2003
After Dark, 2005

Latvia

Norwegian Wood, 2003
A Wild Sheep Chase, 2004

Lithuania

A Wild Sheep Chase, 2003
Hard-Boiled Wonderland and the End of the World, 2004
Dance Dance Dance, 2004
Norwegian Wood, 2005

Netherlands

A Wild Sheep Chase, 1991
Hard-Boiled Wonderland and the End of the World, 1993
South of the Border, West of the Sun, 2001
The Wind-Up Bird Chronicle, 2003
Sputnik Sweetheart, 2005
After Dark, 2006
Kafka on the Shore, 2006
Norwegian Wood, 2007

Norway

A Wild Sheep Chase, 1993
Dance Dance Dance, 1995
Norwegian Wood, 1998
The Wind-Up Bird Chronicle, 1999
South of the Border, West of the Sun, 2000
Hard-Boiled Wonderland and the End of the World, 2001
Kafka on the Shore, 2005

Poland

Norwegian Wood, 1995
Hard-Boiled Wonderland and the End of the World,
    1998
South of the Border, West of the Sun, 2003

Portugal

Norwegian Wood, 2005
Sputnik Sweetheart, 2005

Romania

Norwegian Wood, 2002
A Wild Sheep Chase, 2003
South of the Border, West of the Sun, 2003
Hard-Boiled Wonderland and the End of the World,
    2004
Dance Dance Dance, 2004
The Wind-Up Bird Chronicle, 2004✦
Sputnik Sweetheart, 2004

Russia

A Wild Sheep Chase, 1998
The Wind-Up Bird Chronicle, 2001
Dance Dance Dance, 2002
Hard-Boiled Wonderland and the End of the World,
    2003

Norwegian Wood, 2003
South of the Border, West of the Sun, 2003
Sputnik Sweetheart, 2004
Kafka on the Shore, 2004
After Dark, 2005

Serbia and Montenegro

Dance Dance Dance, 2005

Slovakia

A Wild Sheep Chase, 2004 ✦
Dance Dance Dance, 2006 ✦

Slovenia

Sputnik Sweetheart, 2004
Norwegian Wood, 2005 ✦
South of the Border, West of the Sun, 2005

Spain: Spanish

A Wild Sheep Chase, 1991
The Wind-Up Bird Chronicle, 2001
Sputnik Sweetheart, 2002
South of the Border, West of the Sun, 2003
Norwegian Wood, 2005

Spain: Catalan

Sputnik Sweetheart, 2002
South of the Border, West of the Sun, 2003
Norwegian Wood, 2005 ✦

Sweden

Norwegian Wood, 2003
Underground, 2005

Taiwan

South of the Border, West of the Sun, 1993
Hard-Boiled Wonderland and the End of the World, 1994
A Wild Sheep Chase, 1995
The Wind-Up Bird Chronicle, 1995
Dance Dance Dance, 1996
Underground, 1998
Sputnik Sweetheart, 1999
Kafka on the Shore, 2003
Norwegian Wood, 2004
After Dark, 2005

Thailand

A Wild Sheep Chase, 2003
Norwegian Wood, 2003

South of the Border, West of the Sun, 2003
Hard-Boiled Wonderland and the End of the World,
    2004
Sputnik Sweetheart, 2004

Ukraine

Dance Dance Dance, 2005 ✦

United States

A Wild Sheep Chase, 1989
Hard-Boiled Wonderland and the End of the World,
    1993
Dance Dance Dance, 1994
The Wind-Up Bird Chronicle, 1997
South of the Border, West of the Sun, 1999
Norwegian Wood, 2000
Sputnik Sweetheart, 2001
*Underground: The Tokyo Gas Attack and the Japanese
    Psyche*, 2001
Kafka on the Shore, 2005
After Dark, 2007

About the Contributors

Shozo Fujii is Professor of Chinese Language and Literature at the University of Tokyo. Currently conducting research on "East Asia and Haruki Murakami," he is the author of *Ro Jin jiten* [Lu Xun Encyclopedia], *Chugoku eiga* [Chinese Films], and *Gendai Chugoku bunka tanken* [An Exploration of Modern Chinese Culture], and *Murakami Haruki no naka no Chugoku* [China in Haruki Murakami] among other publications.

Roland Kelts is the author of *Japanamerica: How Japanese Pop Culture Has Invaded the US*, published in both English and Japanese editions. He is also a lecturer at the University of Tokyo and the University of the Sacred Heart Tokyo, an editor of the New York–based literary journal, *A Public Space*, and a columnist for the *Daily Yomiuri*. His fiction and nonfiction writings are published in *Zoetrope: All Story*, *Playboy*, *Salon*, the *Village Voice*, *Psychology Today*, *Doubletake*, *Newsday*, *Animation*, *Cosmopolitan*, *Vogue*, and the *Japan Times*, among many others. Kelts is a recipient of the Jacob K. Javits Fellowship Award in Writing. He lives in New York and Tokyo.

Ivan Sergeevich Logatchov is the Japanese-Russian translator of Murakami's *Portrait in Jazz* and *Ranma ½* by Rumiko Takahashi.

Shinya Machida is a staff writer for the *Yomiuri Shimbun.*

Kim Choon Mie is the Japanese-Korean translator of Murakami's *Kafka on the Shore.* Professor of Japanese Literature and Head of the Research Center of Japanese Studies at Korea University, she has written many books and articles on Japanese literature.

Haruki Murakami is a Japanese novelist whose best-selling books, including *Norwegian Wood, The Wind-Up Bird Chronicle,* and *Kafka on the Shore,* have been translated into over forty languages.

Issey Ogata is a Japanese actor who has appeared in numerous movies, including director Jun Ichikawa's *Tony Takitani.*

Koichi Oi is a staff writer in the Mainichi Newspaper Company's Cultural News Department.

Richard Powers is an American novelist who has received numerous honors including a MacArthur Fellowship, a Lannan Literary Award, the James Fenimore Cooper Prize for Historical Fiction, and the National Book Award, which he received for his 2006 novel *The Echo Maker.*

Jay Rubin is Takashima Research Professor of Japanese Humanities at Harvard University. He has also taught at the University of Chicago and the University of Washington. He has translated into English the fiction of Doppo, Soseki Natsume's *Sanshiro* and *The Miner*, Ryunosuke Akutagawa's *Rashomon and 17 Other Stories*, and Murakami's *The Wind-Up Bird Chronicle* and *Norwegian Wood*.

Inuhiko Yomota is professor of Motion Picture History and Comparative Literature at Meiji Gakuen University and a well-known arts critic. He received the 1998 Suntory Prize for Social Sciences and Humanities for *Eigashi e no shotai* [Introduction to the History of Motion Pictures] and the 2002 Nihon Essayist Club Prize for *Souru no fukei—kioku to hembo* [Landscape of Seoul: Memory and Transformation].

TRANSLATORS

Nozomu Kawamoto, a graduate of the University of Chicago, is currently translation director of the Tokyo-based company Japan Echo, Inc. and a certified Kanze School noh actor.

WordCraft, Inc., established in 1997 by a group of highly experienced professional translators and editors, is a company specializing in translation and editorial services.

Kay Yokota has been a freelance translator since 2003, following five years as an in-house translator and editor at Japan Echo, Inc. She has translated the books *The Secret Techniques of Bonsai, Create Your Own Japanese Garden,* and *The Japanese Skincare Revolution* from Japanese to English and co-translated *Anata no T-shatsu wa doko kara kita no ka* [The Travels of a T-Shirt in the Global Economy] from English to Japanese.